Arthur Asa Berger, PhD

Ocean Travel and Cruising
A Cultural Analysis

ONE WEEK LOAN

Pre-publication
REVIEWS,
COMMENTARIES,
EVALUATIONS . . .

"This is a highly informative, entertaining, yet easy-to-read book on the travel cruise industry. It delves into the psyches of those who use this form of recreation and travel, including the author. He exposes the factors that cause a number of people to be repeat visitors on numerous voyages. Particularly interesting to read about are all the things that are available on the typical cruise. Berger also discusses the fact that the cruise lines use the cheaper labor force of many third-world nations, and explores the market in general."

Percival Darby, MSc
Assistant Professor of Management,
School of Hotel and Travel Management,
Florida International University

"Drawing upon his distinguished background in cultural studies, Berger shares his insights into the meaning and significance of what takes place on cruises. He challenges his readers to consider new perspectives. Can they decode the sign system that surrounds them or navigate the ship as a labyrinth? Are they regressing into the service of the ego or pursuing the paradise myth? Can they overcome the 'agony of choice' when confronted with the assorted gourmet delights of the dining room?

The author provides us with insights into what sets cruises apart from other tourist experiences. Drawing upon a diversity of factors—economics, semiotics, sociology, psychoanalysis, and marketing—he offers readers a fresh and innovative look at cruising as a distinct resort experience."

Brian King, PhD
Head, School of Hospitality,
Tourism and Marketing,
Victoria University, Australia

More pre-publication
REVIEWS, COMMENTARIES, EVALUATIONS . . .

"**D**r. Berger presents an interdisciplinary discussion of the cruise industry for the thinking person. This is an enjoyable social psychology travel guide with a little business management thrown in. A great book for the curious to read a week before embarking on a first cruise or for the frequent cruiser to gain a broader insight into exactly what a cruise experience represents. If you're the kind of person that finds enjoyment by analyzing your environment while on vacation, throw this book into your bag for reading on board. Bon voyage!"

Carl Braunlich, DBA
Associate Professor,
Department of Hospitality
and Tourism Management,
Purdue University,
West Lafayette, Indiana

THHP

The Haworth Hospitality Press®
An Imprint of The Haworth Press, Inc.
New York • London • Oxford

Ocean Travel and Cruising
A Cultural Analysis

Ocean Travel and Cruising
A Cultural Analysis

Arthur Asa Berger, PhD

THHP

The Haworth Hospitality Press®
An Imprint of The Haworth Press, Inc.
New York • London • Oxford

Published by

The Haworth Hospitality Press®, an imprint of The Haworth Press, Inc., 10 Alice Street, Binghamton, NY 13904-1580.

Excerpts from Bob Dickinson and Andy Vladimir, *Selling the Sea: An Inside Look at the Cruise Industry,* copyright 1997. This material is used by permission of John Wiley & Sons, Inc.

Cover design by Jennifer M. Gaska.

Library of Congress Cataloging-in-Publication Data

Berger, Arthur Asa, 1933-
    Ocean travel and cruising : a cultural analysis / Arthur Asa Berger.
        p. cm.
    Includes bibliographical references and index.
    ISBN 0-7890-2197-8 (hardcover : alk. paper)—ISBN 0-7890-2198-6 (softcover : alk. paper)
    1. Ocean travel. 2. Ocean travel—Psychological aspects. 3. Travelers—Psychology. 4. Cruise ships. I. Title.

G550.B417 2004
306.4'8—dc21   2003009812

In memory of Stanley Milgram

ABOUT THE AUTHOR

Arthur Asa Berger is Professor Emeritus of Broadcast and Electronic Communication Arts at San Francisco State University, where he taught from 1965 to 2002. He also taught at the University of Milan in 1963-1964 as a Fulbright scholar and at the Heinrich Heine University in Dusseldorf in 2001 as a Fulbright Senior Specialist. He received his BA in literature and philosophy from the University of Massachusetts and his MA in journalism from the University of Iowa, where he also attended the Writers Workshop. He received his PhD in American studies from the University of Minnesota, where he wrote his dissertation on Al Capp's satirical comic strip, Li'l Abner.

He is the author of fifty books on popular culture, media, humor, and everyday life, and has published more than 100 articles in various journals. His books have been translated into German, Swedish, Italian, Korean, Chinese, and Turkish. He has lectured in a dozen countries during the course of his career. Berger is also an artist and has illustrated a number of his books, as well as books by others. Among his books are *Media Analysis Techniques; Essentials of Mass Communication Theory; Bloom's Morning: Coffee, Comforters and the Secret Meaning of Everyday Life; Ads, Fads and Consumer Culture; An Anatomy of Humor,* and three mysteries that also function as textbooks: *Postmortem for a Postmodernist, The Mass Comm Murders: Five Media Theorists Self-Destruct,* and *Durkheim Is Dead: Sherlock Holmes Is Introduced to Social Theory.*

Dr. Berger is married to Phyllis Wolfson, who teaches philosophy at Diable Valley College. They have two children and two grandchildren. He lives in Mill Valley, California, and can be reached by e-mail at <aberger@sfsu.edu>.

CONTENTS

What gives value to travel is fear. It is the fact that, at a certain moment, when we are so far from our own country . . . we are seized by a vague fear, and this instinctive desire to go back to the protection of old habits. This is the most obvious benefit of travel. At that moment we are feverish but also porous, so that the slightest touch makes us quiver to the depths of our being. . . . This is why we should not say that we travel for pleasure. There is no pleasure in travelling, and I look upon it as an occasion for spiritual testing. Pleasure takes us away from ourselves the same way that distraction, as in Pascal's use of the word, takes us away from God. Travel, which is like a greater and grave science, brings us back to ourselves.

Albert Camus, *Notebooks, 1935-1942*

Preface: The Joke Is on Me!

In 1997 I published a comic mystery novel *Postmortem for a Postmodernist*. In addition to being a mystery story, my book was a textbook on postmodernism and a satire on academia. One of the characters I created was a young French sociologist, Alain Fess, whose claim to fame was that he had written a very serious postmodern analysis of Mall of America in Minnesota.

Alain Fess Speculates

In *Postmortem for a Postmodernist* Fess is writing in his journal and speculating about recent experiences, and, in particular, about a romantic adventure he had in Grasse. He also considers future projects (1997, pp. 138-139):

> I seem, in this entry—and most of my other entries, now that I think about it—to be preoccupied with sex and food. What's so strange about that? Even postmodernists have to eat and take care of their sexual needs. This writing I did tonight: it does have the fissiparous, pastichelike quality that is so characteristic of postmodernity, shown in a linear manner instead of the all-at-onceness of, say, a work of visual art. Is not my time in Grasse paradigmatic of the postmodern emphasis on the carnivalesque, on tourism and places like theme parks, malls, and resorts as central aspects of postmodern cultural and social life? I've done the definitive work on malls in my book on the mall in Minnesota. What next? Maybe cruises would be a good subject? Excellent food, lots of women around. And you get to visit all kinds of exotic places. Very postmodern. Something to think about. I might be able to get a grant and spend a couple of years analyzing cruises?

I was making fun of Fess and all the social scientists who find cushy research projects to work on, many of which are financed by various foundations and institutions, and I thought cruises would be a wonderfully self-indulgent subject for Fess to work on.

Have I Become Alain Fess?

So it came as a big surprise to me when, five years later, I decided that I would write a book on ocean cruises and what has been called "the cruise phenomenon." After I decided to write the book I remembered what I had written in *Postmortem for a Postmodernist* and got a good laugh out of it. I had become, in a sense, the person I had ridiculed—except that, unlike my creation Professor Fess, I am not French and therefore not preoccupied with food and sex! (Or is it sex and food?) At least I don't think I am. Or if so, not any more than most people. A French scholar, who is a friend of mine, thinks I modeled Fess after him and several other French sociologists believe that they are the real models for Fess.

I have written a great number of books, around fifty—probably more than I should have. One editor I know (the one who published *Postmortem for a Postmodernist* and is publishing another mystery, *Durkheim Is Dead: Sherlock Holmes Is Introduced to Sociological Theory*) told me to stop writing. "Find another hobby," he said. My colleagues rib me about my productivity a good deal. I told them, years ago, that I just make things up as I go and throw in charts to fool sociologists. They actually believed me, and when I tell them about a book I've just published they say things such as, "What do you know about *that*?"

I now have a new tack. I tell my colleagues that if I do something once, I make a note about it in my journal. (Like Fess I keep a journal and have been keeping one since 1954.) If I do something twice, I write an article about it. And if I do something three times, I write a book on it.

I have taken three cruises. So I felt that I simply *had* to write this book. Actually, I've taken more than three cruises. My wife and I took a short three-night cruise from Los Angeles to Ensenada a number of years ago on the Norwegian Cruise Line. Then we took a seven-night cruise from Los Angeles to Puerto Vallarta in 1999 on the last sailing of the *Song of America* with Royal Caribbean. In June of 2002 we took a ten-night cruise from San Francisco to Alaska and back on the *Regal Princess* with the Princess line.

We also had taken a three-night boat trip from Shanghai to Hong Kong in 1988 and cruised on the Yangtze River ten years after that, on another trip to China. Both were extremely pleasant but nothing like the ocean cruises that I will be writing about in this book.

Cruisers—Clever or Compulsive?

I finally decided to write about cruises during our trip to Alaska. At lunch one day (breakfasts and lunches were open seating) we sat next to a couple who told us that they had taken twenty-five cruises. I was astounded. I discovered in the course of the cruise that many of the people we dined with had been on ten or fifteen cruises and were very voluble about the differences between the cruise lines, about the best places to go on cruises, about the food on different lines, and many other aspects of cruising.

Are people cruiseaholics? Do some people become hooked on cruising, and if so, why? What are its appeals? Are people who take cruises gullible, or is cruising an extremely rational decision made by tourists who believe, perhaps correctly, that they are getting value for money?

Ocean Travel and Cruising Is an Ethnology

This book is based upon research I've done into the cruise industry and upon observations I've made while cruising—which means it has elements of being a cruise ethnology—that is, it uses ideas, information, and insights that came to me while cruising and deals with experiences I had during some cruises. I discuss, among other things, cruise advertising, the amount of time people spend dining on cruises, the economic aspects of cruising, globalization and the consolidation of the cruise industry, the psyche of cruise takers, Web sites about cruising, and all kinds of other things related to the cruise experience.

In recent years many scholars have become interested in tourism and there are now academic journals, full of often obscure articles by sociologists, psychologists, anthropologists, and other social scientists, devoted to the subject. Someone named Jim Macbeth received a PhD from Murdoch University in Australia for a dissertation titled "Ocean Cruising: A Study of Affirmative Deviance." He argued, as his title suggests, that cruise takers are deviants (that is, different from most people) but in a positive ("affirmative") way.

This book won't be obscure, though in some places—when I offer psychoanalytic interpretations of cruising—you might find it a bit far-fetched. If you have taken cruises, and are an "affirmative deviant," some of the material in the book might even ring a bell with you now and then . . . and maybe more often than that.

Acknowledgments

First of all, let me express my appreciation to Professor Kaye Chon for his assistance in getting *Ocean Travel and Cruising* published. I greatly appreciate his support. I also would like to thank Vance Gulliksen of Carnival Cruises for his help; he was kind enough to have a long conversation with me about the cruising industry and to send me a copy of Bob Dickinson and Andy Vladimir's *Selling the Sea: An Inside Look at the Cruise Industry*. This book was of considerable use to me in writing *Ocean Travel and Cruising*. I discovered to my surprise, when I started doing research on this book, that relatively little of a scholarly nature has been written on ocean cruising. I also want to thank Professor Robert E. Wood for allowing me to use material from his article on economic and globalization aspects of cruising.

I also owe a debt of gratitude to all the passengers aboard the round-trip cruise I took from San Francisco to Alaska on June 8, 2002, who were kind enough to share with me their observations about cruising and discuss, in considerable detail, the various cruises they had taken. I discovered what might be called a certain level of cruise "connoisseurship" among my fellow passengers and learned a great deal from talking with them.

Finally, let me express my appreciation to The Haworth Press, and to the members of its staff who helped me in publishing this book.

Although ships have been a means of transportation since early times, the cruise industry is young. Its purpose is really to provide a resort experience rather than point-to-point transportation. Though the modern-day cruise industry is barely twenty years old, it has established itself as an important component of the United States travel and tourism industry. A study in 1993 by the highly respected U.S. accounting firm Price Waterhouse indicated that the cruise industry has an estimated economic impact on the United States of approximately $14.5 billion annually. It is indirectly responsible for the employment of 450,000 Americans and directly responsible for the employment of 134,000. . . . The cruise industry's performance and satisfaction are the pacesetter for the rest of the travel industry. No other vacation category can touch a cruise for product satisfaction and repeat business.

> Charles R. Goeldner, J.R. Brent Ritchie,
> and Robert W. McIntosh
> *Tourism: Principles, Practices, Philosophies* (Eighth Edition)

Chapter 1

The Economics of Cruising

The cruise industry is an $8 billion industry now, with a 1,400 percent growth rate since 1970. In 1970 approximately 500,000 people took cruises, in 2000, almost 7 million people took cruises, and in 2001, 9.8 million people took cruises. Cruising probably will continue to grow at a very high rate as a large number of new cruise liners have recently been (or will soon be) placed in service. These figures were obtained from The International Council of Cruise Lines, which estimates that by 2010 almost 21 million people will take cruises (see <http://www.iccl.org>). Cruise ships go to 1,800 ports around the world, but the Caribbean and Bahamas are the most popular cruise destinations. In 2000, for example, approximately 46 percent of cruise takers visited the Caribbean.

So cruising is a big business, employing several hundred thousand people in the United States and many others, mostly from third world countries. In this chapter I deal with economic aspects of the cruise industry—what cruises cost, who takes cruises, the incomes of cruise takers, and the problems caused by globalization, among other topics. Some rather surprising statistics are related to the cruising industry, given the image people have (or had, to be more accurate) that cruising is an "elite" form of vacation that only very wealthy people can afford.

CRUISING TO ALASKA: A CASE STUDY

I took a ten-night cruise on the *Regal Princess* to Alaska in June 2002. This cruise started from San Francisco and most of the people on the cruise were people who drove to San Francisco and thus avoided the hassle, and expense, of having to take a plane trip. I asked just about everyone I talked to on the cruise why they took the cruise and almost everybody said they couldn't resist being able to drive to the port and take the cruise and thus avoid the bother of air travel. The cruise line industry is aware of the desire potential passengers have to avoid airports and now are operating cruises from many cities that previously had little or no cruise ship activity.

The *Regal Princess* was scheduled to cruise in the Mediterranean in the summer of 2002 but after the tragedy of September 11, 2001, the ship was repositioned to sail from San Francisco to Alaska. The only other cruise line that sails regularly to Alaska from San Francisco is the Crystal line, which offers twelve-day cruises. Crystal cruises start at around $2,200 per person in inside cabins—that is, more than twice as much as the least expensive cabins on Princess cruises. In 2003, the Princess line will repeat the San Francisco to Alaska and back schedule, with a cruise ship it purchased from the Renaissance Cruise line, a ship that holds only one third as many passengers as the *Regal Princess* does.

On the sailing we took, the least expensive inside cabin on the *Regal Princess* (or stateroom as some cruise lines put it) was $929 per person double occupancy. To that one must add a couple of hundred dollars for port fees and a hundred dollars for tips per person, which means the cruise cost approximately $1,200 or $120 a day per person or a total of $2,400 for two people in the least expensive cabins. An ocean view cabin cost a few hundred dollars more per person and suites cost considerably more, up to thousands of dollars for the cruise. Princess cruises also offered passengers $100 per person shipboard credit—which could be spent for anything except tips—drinks, beauty treatments, tours, or whatever. Drinks cost around $4, so a cruiser who doesn't take tours and likes to drink can drink approximately three drinks a day for "free." This $100 shipboard credit was unusually generous; probably Princess did this because it was anxious about getting people to take the cruise to Alaska. It turns out that every sailing to Alaska was sold out.

Thus, for $1,200, or $1,100 (if you wish to subtract the shipboard credit) per person, you could sail to Alaska, visit ports in Victoria, Juneau, Sitka, and Ketchikan, eat three gourmet meals a day (or more if you wanted), enjoy afternoon tea, see three elaborate stage shows (and other shows with a harmonica player, comedian, magician, and singer—there was a show every night in the theater), go dancing every night, drink free champagne at a party the captain threw—all of this for around the price of an airline ticket from San Francisco to Europe during the high season. If you booked the tours that Princess offered, it could cost you a good deal more, but many people contented themselves with sightseeing in the various stops the ship made rather than booking tours.

Cruises can offer a disciplined person (and maybe those who aren't so disciplined) considerable value for money and are generally regarded as worth what they cost by people who take cruises. A friend of mine once explained to me one of the benefits of cruising: "If you went to a restaurant and ordered the kind of meals you have on a cruise, it would cost you a small fortune. And on a cruise ship, these meals are free." He was right. The kind of breakfast you can have on a cruise could easily cost $20 in a hotel. The four- or five-course lunches and six- or seven-course dinners could cost $50 or $75, or more, in a decent restaurant.

One reason cruise lines can offer such elaborate dining is because of economies of scale and because little waste occurs. Cruise lines can serve passengers steaks, roast beef, lobsters, shrimp, escargot, Alaskan crab legs, caviar, and fancy desserts for relatively little money—as little as $8 a day on budget lines, around $15 a day on premium lines, and around $25 a day on luxury lines. I obtained these figures from *Selling the Sea* (Dickinson and Vladimir, 1997); they are quite incredible and no doubt much lower than many people would imagine. Since *Selling the Sea* was written in 1997, the figures may be a bit low.

Carnivores and Omnivores on Carnival

To give an idea of the scale of these purchases, a Carnival Cruise Line (n.d.) press release detailed the weekly food and beverage consumption on all Carnival ships during a typical week, as presented in the following list.

> 37,000 pounds of tenderloin
> 78,000 pounds of chicken
> 12,440 Cornish game hens

    7,570 whole ducks
368,000 shrimp
  12,300 pounds of veal
  65,000 hot dogs
  87,100 hamburgers
    9,900 pounds of ham
    7,500 pounds of salmon
    4,190 pounds of nova (smoked salmon)
  15,500 pounds of lobster
  17,370 pounds of coffee
  12,230 gallons of milk
  19,690 bagels
    1,450 pounds of grits
  69,070 individual boxes of breakfast cereals
137,180 tomatoes
210,400 potatoes
329,560 cans of soft drinks
    5,780 gallons of soda from the bar fountains
426,980 domestic and imported beers
  23,470 bottles of champagne and sparkling wines
  52,297 bottles of wine
  12,640 bottles of Scotch

Obviously, an enormous amount of food and drink is consumed by
the passengers on seventeen Carnival ships in a typical week. How
Carnival knows that it used exactly 19,690 bagels and 137,180 tomatoes is beyond me, but I will give their cooks and accountants the benefit of the doubt and assume that they keep very detailed records of
everything they serve. Not only do they keep detailed records of what
they serve, cruise lines can anticipate very accurately what passengers are going to order at every meal and thus can avoid waste.

    Dickinson and Vladimir (1997) explain why cruise lines can spend
so little on food. In the restaurant business food costs should run between 25 and 30 percent of the selling price, while a mass market
cruise line has costs of around $10 a day. A restaurant or hotel com-
peting with a cruise line would have to charge between $33 to $40 per
person for the same food array, which is impossible for them to do. In
addition, cruise lines have another advantage—they serve identical
meals on all ships in their fleets.

CRUISES COMPARED TO LAND-BASED VACATIONS

In *Selling the Sea* (1997), authors Bob Dickinson, president of Carnival, and Andy Vladimir, a market researcher, compare a budget cruise and a land vacation for a couple on a per diem basis in the chart (which I have slightly modified) that follows:

	Cruise ($)	Land ($)
Transportation	Presumed comparable for both	
Room	160	85
Port charges/taxes	28	11
Breakfast	Included	10
Lunch	Included	16
Dinner	Included	32
Drinks	6	10
Tips	10	5
Snacks	Included	6
Activities	Included	17
Entertainment	Included	12
TOTAL	204	204

Dickinson and Vladimir did a bit of fudging in this chart to make the cruise end up costing as much as a land-based vacation, but the figures are reasonably accurate. Many motels cost less than $85 a day but the average couple probably spends more than $58 for food and snacks. The chart assumes that a couple on a cruise has one drink per day, doesn't gamble, and doesn't "splurge" and take any tours at the ports the ship visits, among other things.

But even with these caveats, the fact is that a couple on a cruise will eat much better than a couple on land, will have the experience of being on a ship (which many people value highly), will most likely have better entertainment, and won't have to do any driving! In addition, cruises provide more opportunities for social interaction; the couple on the land-based vacation will probably spend most of their time by themselves, unlike cruises, where passengers dine with others and have many other opportunities to socialize.

The purpose of the chart is to counter the "sticker shock" people may experience when they find out what a cruise costs. The expenses on a cruise are, for the most part, up front. Actually, anyone who reads travel sections of newspapers or magazines or searches the Internet knows what cruises will cost since the prices of cruises are advertised—along with port fees. These advertisements always use the lowest price, or "inside" cabins, when they quote prices, so people contemplating taking a cruise have a pretty good idea of what we might call an "entry level" cruise will cost. Arthur Frommer (n.d.), the well-known travel writer, suggested that people taking cruises book inside cabins as a way of economizing, especially since all the social "action" on cruise ships takes place in the public spaces.

OTHER WAYS CRUISE LINES MAKE MONEY

The basic cost of the cruise we took to Alaska (in the least expensive inside cabin) was about $1,200 per person, including port charges and tips. But cruise lines make money in many other ways. Not only do cruise lines sell the sea—that is, sell people on taking cruises— once passengers are on cruises they find many other buying opportunities.

1. *Tours at ports visited.* Some of these tours are extremely expensive, running to hundreds of dollars, such as taking a helicopter and landing on a glacier. Many people who take cruises are questing for adventure and thus are willing to "splurge" and spend money on these land tours. They were all sold out on the voyage my wife and I took.
2. *Alcoholic beverages and soft drinks.* Alcoholic beverages averaged around $4 each and soft drinks were a couple of dollars for a can and $1 from a bar.
3. *Gambling.* The casino on the ship was another source of revenue, though casinos do not generate the amount of money most people think they do. Only a third of the people on cruise liners

gamble, and they spend approximately $10 a day. The other passengers watch.

4. *Phoning home.* This service, which uses satellites, can be very expensive, running as much as $15 a minute on some lines.

5. *Internet cafes.* It is possible to use the Internet on ships nowadays and many of the new ships have Internet cafes . . . or other ways of accessing the Internet. This is less expensive than using phones, but not cheap.

6. *Art auctions.* During our tour we were amazed to see the interest passengers had in the art auctions, which seemed to be going on endlessly and were very well attended.

7. *Photographs.* Passengers on cruise lines are photographed when they get on the ship, when they dine, sometimes when they leave the dining room, when they are dressed for formal dinners, and many other times. Nobody is required to purchase any of the photographs, but many people do and the lines make a great deal of money from this operation.

8. *Beauty salons and spas.* The beauty salon and spa services on the *Regal Princess* (including mud wraps, massages, facials, and so on) were fully booked the day after we left San Francisco. The Princess line also charged $10 per session for yoga classes.

Since many people regard taking a cruise as what Dickinson and Vladimir (1997) call a "renewal" experience, they are willing to spend additional money for all of the items previously listed. It is easy to spend a great deal of money in addition to the initial cost of the cruise, but you don't have to, and I noticed that many people on our cruise didn't take any tours or excursions at all, but wandered around the ports on their own. Some cruisers, who had been to Alaska many times, didn't even get off the ship.

In reading reviews of various ships and trips on cruise Web sites, I noticed that in a number of cases people who took cruises were celebrating anniversaries and other happy events and thus wanted to do everything and see everything, and money was no object. That is, a large number of these reviews indicated that because these people were taking what they considered to be a "vacation of a lifetime," they were prepared to spend freely—on suites rather than cabins and on tours and excursions. A couple at our table said they had budgeted

$800 for tours at the ports we visited, which amounted to $200 per port.

At the end of their discussion of on-board revenue opportunities, Dickinson and Vladimir (1997) point out that most cruise lines are not making money. The reason for this, the reason that they are operating at a loss, they suggest, is because they have poor management. Bob Dickinson is the president of Carnival lines, the most successful cruise line in the industry. Carnival also owns Holland America, Windstar, Costa, Seabourn, and Cunard and recently purchased Princess lines. Some people who sail on the other lines Carnival owns have no idea that they are sailing on a line owned by Carnival. It is the 800-pound gorilla in the cruise world.

CRUISE CATEGORIES

In some cases, it is difficult to determine in which category a cruise line belongs, but what follows (adapted from *Selling the Sea,* Dickinson and Vladimir, 1997)) is a pretty good approximation of the way cruise lines are classified by people in the industry. Carnival-owned lines are in italics.

Budget	Contemporary	Premium	Specialty	Luxury
Commodore	*Carnival*	*Princess*	*Windstar*	Sea Goddess
Fantasy	Premier	Holland Amer.	Club Med	*Seabourn*
Seawind	Royal Caribbean	Celebrity	Pearl	*Cunard*
Dolphin	*Costa*	Delta Queen	Orient	Silversea
Regal	Norwegian (NCL)			Crystal

Crystal lines is a problem here because it straddles the luxury category and advertises itself as such. I placed it in the luxury category even though it was not there in the original chart. Certain other lines such as Norwegian and Royal Caribbean are upgrading themselves and trying to reposition themselves as premium lines. Crystal is owned by a Japanese company and Royal Caribbean, which battled with Carnival to purchase Princess lines, also owns Celebrity cruises.

CONSOLIDATION OF THE CRUISE INDUSTRY

In an article on consolidation in the cruise industry, sociologist Robert E. Wood deals with the difficulties cruise lines pose to governments that seek to regulate them. He writes in his paper "Globalization at Sea: Cruise Ships and the Deterritorialization of Capital, Labor, and Place" (2000, pp. 8-9):

> Because the bulk of both its physical capital and its labor force are at sea, cruise companies have been able to gain further independence from regulation by incorporating themselves in developing countries that make a business of not regulating business. Except for banks and certain other financial institutions, this does not offer much of an advantage for most land-based companies, whose plants and workers come under the sovereignty of the nation in which they are physically located. However, in the United States, federal tax code exempts from taxation foreign corporations' income from ships and aircraft. Virtually all airlines are incorporated in a home country that imposes taxes on their international operations. The major cruise companies are not; they are incorporated in countries which refrain from taxing and regulating them almost entirely. They are unique in their liberation from taxation and the other traditional constraints of political and legal space.

Cruise lines, Wood argues, are extraterritorial powers and because they can move around at will, it is difficult for countries to deal with them. By incorporating in small islands with lax tax laws (becoming, that is, Flags of Convenience), cruise lines save millions of dollars on taxes in the United States, and can exploit people from the third world, who work on these ships for very low wages.

This may be changing, however. Recently, an American court ruled in favor of workers on a cruise line who sued for wages due them for working overtime. Their contract was for seventy hours of work a week and work in excess of that was ruled overtime.

Wood addresses another aspect of the cruise industry, what he called the "deterritorialization" effects of globalization in the cruise industry (2000, p. 9):

As in other sectors, the globalization of the cruise industry has led to increased concentration in the industry. The pace of mergers, acquisitions, and bankruptcies in the industry has been dizzying over the past two decades. Carnival Corporation, which in 1980 owned a mere three ships, with 3,950 berths, has in the meantime acquired Holland America, Seabourn, Costa, Windstar, and Cunard lines, and grown to become the world's largest cruise company, with a total of 43 ships and a potential passenger capacity over 50,000; it also has part interest in Airtours' Sun Cruises.

The cruise industry, like many other industries, is undergoing rapid consolidation, and if things continue to develop in the future as they have in the past, soon there will be only a few giant cruise companies that own all, or most of, the cruise lines. Carnival lines recently beat out Royal Caribbean in the battle to purchase Princess cruise lines, which will give Carnival and the other lines it owns more than 43 percent of the $11 billion cruise market. When the final arrangements for the purchase of Princess lines have been completed, Carnival and its subsidiaries will have seventy-three ships and approximately 115,000 beds. The next largest cruise company, Royal Caribbean, has about 24 percent of the cruise market, and is a great deal smaller than Carnival.

Wood discusses the impact of the consolidation of the cruise industry in terms of the power that cruise lines have to force weak countries, which desperately want their business, to acquiesce to their demands. He explains (Wood 2000, pp. 9-10):

This concentration has accentuated the imbalance of power that already exists between the cruise companies and most of the countries of their ports of call. The companies are not only few, thus reducing the capacity of port countries to play them off against each other, but they are also well-organized, e.g., in International Council of Cruise Lines and the Cruise Lines International Association. The threat to leave—carried out much more easily and frequently than even in *maquiladora* and export processing zone industries—has kept port fees to a bare minimum.

Wood points out the enormous amount of power these lines have over many of the countries at their ports of call, especially in the Caribbean.

Only 13 percent of the American public has taken cruises; the question remains about how successful the cruise lines will be in attracting people from the remaining 87 percent of the public. The industry must find ways to reach these people because a large number of new cruise ships are being built; these ships will greatly expand the number of cabins available. As the Cruise Lines International Association (CLIA) (n.d.) points out, in the 1980s some forty new cruise ships were built. In the 1990s eighty-two new cruise ships were built and in the next five years fifty-two new cruise ships will enter service.

In *Selling the Sea,* Dickinson and Vladimir (1997) suggest that a danger of overcapacity exists, especially at the higher so-called premium levels. This overcapacity has been caused by premium lines building too many ships, by new lines being created in the premium status, and by other lines upgrading themselves to premium status. Carnival lines has made an enormous amount of money by targeting the average middle-class or lower-middle-class cruise taker. In some years it reported 110 percent occupancy. This figure reflects the fact that it is often possible to have more than two people in a cabin—as, for example, when a couple travels with two children.

Winner Take All

America, some culture critics have suggested, is a "winner take all" society. Increasing consolidation is taking place in many industries (though these consolidations haven't always worked out the way they were supposed to) as large corporations purchase smaller ones and grow even larger. Since free-enterprise capitalism is based on the notion of competition, this increased consolidation, which lessens competition, presents problems to our free-enterprise system. In the cruise industry, one company—Carnival—now dominates the industry, with ships in every category except budget. If the cruise industry were a traditional industry, Carnival could raise prices, but because only a small percentage of Americans take cruises, and because there still are other players in the industry, including Royal Caribbean, which is also very large, the traditional laws of economics do not seem to apply.

One interesting question is—how much profit are these lines making? How much does it cost to run a typical cruise liner? It must be very profitable for some lines, otherwise they would not be investing billions of dollars in new gigantic cruise ships. Significant overcapacity is now leading to lower prices, since it is much more profitable to lower prices and fill a ship than to sail with a half empty ship. Consider the following e-mail message I received on July 24, 2002, from cruisemates.com, a Web site devoted to cruises:

NEWS FROM CRUISEMATES—July 24, 2002
(CruiseMates is an interactive cruise guide. NOT A TRAVEL AGENCY. *National Geographic Traveler* recently rated Cruise-Mates as the top cruise site on the Internet.)

Egads, I never thought I'd see the kinds of low fares that are available now on fall cruises. In a random survey of travel agencies, I found seven-night sailings on Holland America in the Caribbean, and on Princess in Mexico, starting at $599, including port charges. A 14-day Celebrity South America cruise begins at $1,000, and Radisson Seven Seas Cruises is discounting Radisson Diamond Europe cruises by 70 percent. And hey, it's still July! If you can't wait until September, you'll find some very good deals on August departures.

The reason cruise prices are so low is the enormous amount of overbuilding by the cruise industry. In 2002 alone, 14 new vessels have—or will—enter service. This comes on top of a steady stream of new ships carrying up to 3,500 passengers that have rolled out of shipyards over the past five years. What's more, demand has softened because the stock market is in the tank and some folks are still afraid to fly.

My advice is to grab these rates now, because if you think they're a great deal, so will a lot of other people. Cruise ships go out full these days—the cruise lines just don't make much money. Also, upgrade to a balcony cabin or mini-suite while you have the chance.

This e-mail message argues that overbuilding by cruise lines has made cruises even cheaper than usual, and suggests that people planning on taking cruises sign up for "incredible bargains" right away. Whether the lines don't make any money is, I would suggest, a questionable matter. Logic would suggest that cruise lines wouldn't keep on building new ships if they weren't making a profit or couldn't foresee making a profit in the near future.

EXPLOITATION OF WORKERS ON CRUISE SHIPS?

In his article on cruising, sociologist Robert Wood deals with the changes in the ethnicity of workers that have taken place in the cruise industry in recent years. He writes (2000, pp. 11-12):

> Below the officer caste is a category of staff, one whose ethnic composition is rapidly changing. Historically this category was filled by North Americans and Western Europeans, and on the most expensive luxury ships, positions down to the level of waiters and cabin stewards are still filled this way. Increasingly, however, non-Western workers are being recruited for these staff positions. Below this is the crew, on most ships in recent years almost entirely from Asia, Eastern Europe, or Central America and the Caribbean. The ethnic/racial line between staff and crew has become blurred, however, and the term "international" has come to be applied to all non-European, non-North American cruise ship workers (East Europeans occupy a somewhat ambiguous place in this schema, but generally fall into the "international" category). Several cruise lines take pains to stress that their international staff is "European-trained." The widespread use of the term "international" in the cruise industry to apply only to labor migrants from poorer, mostly third world, countries is a revealing semantic reflection of the inequities of deterritorialization. Employees from richer countries do not lose their nationalities.

How much people who work on cruise ships earn depends, of course, on what kind of work they do. Workers who interact with passengers—and who must know English—earn more than ordinary seamen and others who may not know English. Wood offers detailed information on the wages of cruise workers (2000, p. 12):

> For the "international" crew, cruise ship wages are often princely compared to what they could earn at home. Most are nonethe-

less far below the rates the companies would have to pay if they had to meet minimum wage and other standards in the countries where they are headquartered. Many positions depend almost entirely on tips. According to Sea Cruise Enterprises (1999), an agency that specializes in cruise ship job placement, cabin stewards, bar waiters and waitresses, dining room waiters and waitresses, wine stewards, and busboys all earn $50 a month and rely mainly on tips, which can range between $1,000 and $1,500. Lower-level cooks' helpers and trainees, who receive no tips, earn $500-800, cleaners $350-500, and ordinary (OS) and able-bodied seamen (ABS), $500-800 per month.

Obviously, workers on these ships who do not get tips aren't well paid. Many of these workers come from countries where endemic unemployment and underemployment exists and probably feel that even a low-paying job is better than no job at all. That would explain why they are working on cruise ships.

My calculations concerning how much waiters, assistant waiters, and stewards make are somewhat different from those of Professor Wood. On the *Regal Princess,* we were told that tips should average $10 a day: waiters and stewards should get $3.50 a day and assistant waiters $2.00 or $2.50. We could give $5 or $10 to the head waiter and maitre d'. My waiter had responsibility for eighteen people at dinner for the first serving and presumably the same number of people for the second serving. I don't know how many cabins our room steward serviced, but let's assume he took care of fifteen cabins or thirty people. Following are the figures, then, for these workers for the ten-night trip:

Waiter	$3.50 per day per person	$1,260 for ten nights	$3,780 a month
Room steward	$3.50 per day per person	$1,050 for ten nights	$3,150 a month
Assistant waiter	$2.50 per day per person	$900 for ten nights	$2,700 a month

These jobs pay, in third-world terms, relatively high salaries due to the tips passengers give these workers. The jobs are very difficult, with incredibly long hours. My waiter on the *Regal Princess* said he had been working for Princess lines for twelve years. He typically signs a contract for ten months, he added. Our waiter on the Royal Caribbean cruise we took from Los Angeles to Puerto Vallarta was from India and told us he was building a large house in India with the money he had made working on cruise ships.

Clearly, most of the workers on the cruise lines are working at very low and, by American standards, exploitative wages. The cruise companies claim that they cannot pay higher salaries and make a decent profit. It would be best, perhaps, if the cruise lines paid their workers a bit more money and made smaller profits, but how to be fair to workers and to stockholders is a matter on which I cannot speak with authority, especially since a number of cruise lines are struggling to survive.

CONCLUSION

The cruising industry is a very complicated one. New cruise ships cost hundreds of millions of dollars and are being built at a rapid pace—one that may be too fast for the cruise industry's own good, given the state of the American economy. The day after September 11, 2001, large numbers of people canceled their cruises and the industry has been struggling to return to a more normal state of affairs. This seems to be happening and bookings are now close to what they were before the September 11 tragedy.

Dickinson and Vladimir (1997) argue that the most basic mistake the cruise lines are making is in upscaling themselves and fighting for an increase in their share of the cruise-taking market rather than working to enlarge the number of people who take cruises. This, they suggest, is having devastating consequences because the lines lose a large number of potential first-time cruisers, which means the industry isn't growing as rapidly as it might. How to reach the noncruising 87 percent of the American public is the big problem!

Although the tourist need not be consciously aware of this, the thing he goes to see is society and its works. The societal aspect of tourist attractions is hidden behind their fame, but this fame cannot change their origin in social structure. Given the present sociohistorical epoch, it is not a surprise to find that tourists believe sightseeing is a leisure activity, and fun, even when it requires more effort and organization than many jobs. In a marked contrast to the grudging acquiescence that may characterize the relation of the individual to his industrial work, individuals happily embrace the attitudes and norms that lead them into a relationship with society through the sightseeing act. In being presented as a valued object through a so-called "leisure" activity that is thought to be "fun," society is renewed in the heart of the individual through warm, open, unquestioned relations, characterized by a near absence of alienation when compared with other contemporary relationships.

Dean MacCannell, *The Tourist: A New Theory of the Leisure Class*

Chapter 2

Signs at Sea: The Semiotics of Cruising

Tourism has been described by semioticians (semiotics is the science of signs) as the "consumption" of signs by people who want to see the great buildings and interesting sites the world has to offer, and who often take pictures of themselves in front of these places. But what's a sign? How do signs communicate?

A PRIMER ON SEMIOTICS

For those not familiar with semiotics, it deals with how people find meaning in life. Semiotics is based on the notion that just about everything we see and do is connected with sending and receiving messages—which take the form of signs. *A sign is anything that can be used to stand for something else.* That is, a sign represents something to someone. Words are signs. Buildings are signs. Facial expressions are signs. Being blonde is a sign. A flag is a sign. For semioticians, the world is made up of signs. These signs, as one important semiotic theorist, Ferdinand de Saussure (1966), argued, are comprised of two connected parts—two sides of the same coin, so to speak. On one side we have a *signifier,* which takes the form of a sound or image or object (and buildings and cruise liners are objects from this perspective), and on the other side we find a *signified,* which is the concept or meaning that sound or object has. For example, the Eiffel Tower is a signifier and what it signifies is Paris or France and cruise liners are signifiers and what they signify, broadly speaking, is pleasure and luxury.

de Saussure argued that we need to learn what the signifiers mean; they are arbitrary and based on convention and thus can have many different meanings and their meanings can change over time. Words are signs and words often change their meaning over the years. This also applies to cruises. They used to signify activities of elites and for many people, they still do.

Tourists are people who, from the semiotic perspective, want to see the world, or as much of it as they possibly can, given their finances and interests. We want to *see* the world—to visit the best and most desirable places, to go to countries where people do things differently from the way we do them. We want to sample different foods and drink different drinks. To prove that we've done these things, and to have something to remind us of our adventures, we record our travels by taking photographs or making videos.

It is not unusual to see tourists taking video shots of famous buildings and talking into their cameras: "It's July fourteenth and we're here in Paris at the Bastille . . ." Seeing—that is, being "there"—is a big part of tourism. Immersing ourselves in a different culture, if only for a short time, refreshes us and recharges our batteries.

Another theorist of semiotics, Charles Peirce (1977), provides ideas of importance. He argued that we find meaning in signs (and thus in the world) in three ways: some signs resemble what they stand for; he called these signs *icons*. You see icons everywhere—on roads, on computer screens, and in airports. You don't have to be able to read to know what an icon means. Think, for example, of the icon of a man—usually a highly simplified representation—used in airports and other public places to show that a door or an opening leads to a man's rest room.

The second kind of sign creates meaning by showing connections between things; Peirce called this kind of sign an *index*. When we see smoke, we assume there is fire, and generally there is fire. So smoke is indexically connected to fire. When we go to the doctor and describe our symptoms, the doctor uses these symptoms to try to figure out what is wrong with us. What makes things difficult here is that a given symptom can have, in some cases, a number of different causes. The third kind of sign called by Peirce a *symbol,* must be learned. For example, a flag is a symbol, but you are not born knowing that a flag with fifty stars and alternating red and white stripes represents the United States. You have to be taught this. According to semioticians, we spend a great deal of time generating signs (the clothes we wear, the cars we drive) and interpreting signs (the clothes others wear, the cars others drive).

THE CRUISE SHIP AS A SIGN SYSTEM

The physical beauty of cruise ships functions as a signifier for people of the wonderful experiences they can expect on the ship when they are passengers, and of the escape from life on the land and its many routines. It is for that reason that cruise lines use their ships prominently in their catalogs and advertising. Ships are streamlined and elegant and handsome in their own right, but they also contain enough detail—in the windows, the various decks, the swimming pools, the passageways, the smokestacks, the portholes, and balconied suites—to make them also visually interesting. Cruise liners have elegance and something of the industrial aesthetic that combine to make them beautiful and interesting objects. Many smaller signs exist within the large and complex sign we know of as a cruise ship.

Ships traditionally have been personified as feminine. The line I traveled on, the Princess line, was made famous by the television series *The Love Boat*. Perhaps ships are portrayed as feminine because they are incorporative, taking in people just as females are, psychoanalytically speaking, incorporative. (A well-known psychologist, the late Erik Erikson, once conducted a very interesting experiment. He asked little boys and girls to play with blocks. The boys built towers and the girls built enclosures, leading him to suggest that males are penetrating beings and females are incorporative.) Thus, we traditionally talk about ships using feminine terms—she's a beautiful liner, she's got very elegant lines, and so on. We do this because we associate the feminine with beauty.

Therefore, ships can be looked upon as very complicated signs, or, to be more accurate, sign systems, in which numerous other signs speak to passengers. Often, smaller signs are found within larger ones. We derive a certain amount of pleasure from being on a beautiful ship, and I've noticed in reading reviews people make of their cruise experiences that they often comment on the beauty of the cruise liners they were on. I traveled to Alaska on the *Regal Princess,* which was designed by a famous Italian architect, Renzo Piano. He designed the ship to have a profile something like a dolphin. The negative part of the Piano design is that the *Regal Princess* doesn't have a walking deck that completely circles the ship, so people who like to walk the decks on ships to get exercise can't do the kind of walking they can do on other ships.

What the cruise lines sell, generally speaking—and I'll say more about this in my analysis of cruise advertising—is luxury, elegance, refinement, and pleasure. They also sell freedom and escape. Let's consider some areas where they use signs to do this.

Cabins Also Known As Staterooms

The cabins in which passengers sleep do not offer a great deal of opportunity for cruise lines to suggest elegance, except for those cabins with large picture windows, which enable the cruise companies to use spectacular scenery and vistas to help connect cabins with that beauty. For the most part, cabins are relatively simple rooms that do not afford much opportunity for beautification. The lines do provide thick towels to generate a sense of luxury. The cabins are kept very clean by unobtrusive stewards, who do one other thing to give passengers a sense of high living and luxury—they provide room service. That is, they bring breakfasts (and other meals) to passengers who want to eat in their cabins.

All you have to do is fill out a form stating what you'd like to have for breakfast and leave it on the cabin door the night before. This room service suggests to passengers that they are being pampered and living the way wealthy people do . . . or the way we think they do. Being served breakfast in bed is a sign of being special and also of love, as when children serve their mothers in bed on Mother's Day.

On cruises, we are all kings and queens for a week, or however long the cruises last. If the cabin is the moral equivalent of the bedroom, the dining hall is the equivalent of the dining room, and that is where cruise lines intensify the passengers' sense of living luxuriously. The ship we traveled on was the *Regal Princess*—regal and princess are both terms for royalty and, by implication, aristocratic taste. The connotations of the name suggest, perhaps, that the *Regal Princess* is a kind of royal castle—good enough for royalty.

Dining Rooms

The Palm Court dining room on my Alaska cruise was a very handsome space. The tables were all covered with linen with starched napkins for the diners. The waiters and assistant waiters wore crisp, clean uniforms. The table had many different knives and forks and spoons, suggesting a many-coursed meal was awaiting the diner.

Consider, for example, the captain's gala dinner. Not only were different dishes available, but also the language used to describe some of the dishes was interesting. Thus, the caviar was served on an "ice throne," the shrimp were "jumbo," and the chicken consommé was "double." The pheasant—itself a signifier of gourmet food—was "royal." Sevruga Malossol caviar, a signifier of being elite and sophisticated, was one appetizer choice. (Sevruga caviar is not the "best" caviar and it isn't in the same class as Beluga caviar, which is served on luxury cruises, but it is good enough to signify luxury.)

The following is the menu from the Captain's Gala Dinner on the *Regal Princess* cruise I was on.

Appetizers
Caspian Sevruga Malossol Caviar on Ice Throne
Jumbo Shrimp Cocktail with Calypso Sauce
Golden Fresh Fruit Collections with Kirsch

Soups
Double Chicken Consommé with Vermicelli
Roasted Garlic Bisque with Rosemary
Jellied Beef Consommé Madrilène with Celery Julienne

Salad
Radicchio, Boston Lettuce, and Tomato
Thousand Island, Balsamic Vinaigrette, or Low-Fat House Italian Dressing

Pasta
Ravioli Con Salsa de Funghi Porcini
Pasta Squares filled with Meat in a Creamy Mushroom Sauce

Entrées
Baby Turbot and Saffron Mayonnaise
Sautéed Fish with Beans, Bell Pepper Boats, and Crusty New Potatoes
Broiled Lobster Tail on the Shell with Melted Lemon Butter and Rice Pilaf
Royal Pheasant in Pan Juices

Oven Roast with Brussels Sprouts, Champignon, and Parisienne Potatoes

Beef Wellington

Puff Pastry-Wrapped Tenderloin in a Black Truffle Madeira Sauce with Baby Vegetables and Duchess Potatoes

Desserts

Frozen Mango Yogurt with Strawberry and Pistachios

A Duet of White and Dark Chocolate Mousses with Chocolate Curls

Lemon Lime Soufflé with Orange Sabayon

From the Ship's Ice Cream Fountain

Watermelon Sorbet

Coffee Ice Cream

Rocky Road Ice Cream

Assorted International Cheese and Crackers

Parmesan

Cheddar

Brie

Fontina

The number of different choices, the kinds of food served (caviar, lobster, Beef Wellington), and the language used to describe many of the dishes all contributed to a sense of discrimination, refinement, and luxury. The diners were expected to know that champignon meant mushrooms and what sorbet is. In addition, the fact that the dining hall had days devoted to different national cuisines—English, French, and Italian—enhanced passengers' sense of being cosmopolitan world travelers. In fact, many of them were.

The service was superb. The waiters were extremely efficient and very helpful, and if asked, would make suggestions about what was "best" on the menu. The assistant waiters kept everyone's water glass filled and whisked away plates when a given course was finished. In addition, the number of plates used was extraordinary. Everything was done the way it is done in fine restaurants, which made dining a very pleasant experience.

If the dining room was refined and sophisticated, the Café del Sol buffet restaurant on the twelfth deck of the ship was decidedly proletarian. A great deal of food and many choices were provided, but the dishes lacked the elegance of the meals in the dining room. In addition, one served oneself and ate at Formica tables. Interestingly enough, quite a few people preferred eating in the Café del Sol, and it was always full. Personally speaking, it wasn't to my taste and I ate all my meals, except for lunch the day we boarded the ship (I didn't know the dining hall was open) in the Palm Court dining room. Possibly, some passengers weren't familiar with some of the cuisines and were somewhat anxious about ordering dishes from the menu. I would suggest that the Palm Court was for dining and the Café del Sol was for eating, though that may be oversimplifying matters.

The Regal Princess *As Museum*

Regal Princess brochures indicated the ship contained $2 million worth of paintings and artwork, suggesting an elite nature and, in a sense, a floating museum. Rather large works of art hung on the walls on the landings of various stairwells in the ship. I noticed a large work by Robert Motherwell and some other rather handsome paintings by artists with whom I was not familiar.

These works can be contrasted with the nondescript paintings one finds in most hotel rooms, suggesting that the experience of being on the *Regal Princess* "museum" (and other cruise ships do the same, with millions of dollars worth of art on them) was an elevated and enriching one. What one gains from having the opportunity to see original works of fine art is the "aura" of the artist and of the work. One can experience the spirit and vitality of the painter and the beauty of the work, which is not transferable, so many theorists argue, in copies of such works. In reality, in today's market, $2 million doesn't buy much in the way of great art, but it is possible to buy many very fine original works of art for that amount of money. These works of art do lend a sense of enrichment and elevation to the cruising experience. (The art on the walls of the ship contrasted greatly with the schlock art being sold at the art auctions.)

A number of examples of what might be called "food art" also decorated the ship—clever ice carvings and displays of food turned into sculptures, generally in the lobby where one entered the dining hall. In addition, a great deal of attention was given to the presentation of food at each meal, which heightened the sense that being on the cruise was something rather special. This notion was enhanced by the table settings: the starched tablecloth and napkins, the glassware, the silverware, the serving plates, and so on. At some meals, strolling musicians gave the meals an added touch of refinement.

Dress Codes and Class

The officers on cruise ships wear handsome white uniforms with various insignia that reflect their rank in the ship's command hierarchy. Every officer has a place in the chain of command. Cruise ships, like all ships, are hierarchical in nature and, in truth, quite authoritarian. The captain commands and all others on the staff obey. This contrasts with the seeming classlessness of the passengers. You don't know from the way people dress who has the very expensive suites and who has inside cabins. The passengers, as a rule, dress very casually, except for those evenings when the dinners are formal and male passengers wear tuxedos or dark suits and female passengers wear evening gowns or fancy dresses. For men who don't own a tuxedo but want to dress up, it is possible to rent one on the cruise.

One of the problems the cruise industry faces is that many people still have the idea that cruises are terribly expensive and just for very wealthy "elites" and that ordinary middle-class people, even if they could afford cruises, would find it awkward and unpleasant to be with such people. That is, some people are afraid that the wealthy passengers on board will look down on them. Cruises used to be for the elites years ago, and were far too expensive for the average person, but this has all changed and on a typical cruise you can find people from many different socioeconomic classes.

The very wealthy maintain social distance on cruises by choosing so-called "luxury" cruises, on lines such as Seabourn and Silversea, where cruises tend to be several weeks in length and the advertised price of around $800 a day per passenger keeps most people away. I can recall a conversation I had with someone I met at lunch on the *Regal Princess*. He told me he'd been on many cruise lines, including the Crystal lines, which advertises itself as a luxury line and is ranked as the best large ship cruise line by many travel publications.

"What was it like?" I asked.

"I didn't like it that much," he replied. "The food wasn't any better than on this ship, except there was more caviar. And the people were too standoffish."

Social scientists have discovered that wealthy people often dress down so that their class level will be hidden, so it is isn't unusual to see people from the upper income levels dressing in blue jeans and other casual clothing. On most cruise ships, class distinctions are not evident; a person on an inside cabin may dine with someone in the most expensive suite on the ship.

The newer cruise ships can be as large as 110,000 tons. These ships now have huge atriums full of shops and some of the cabins face the atriums rather than the sea. These megaliners were designed to keep people entertained on the ship. The theory is that it's more profitable for the cruise line to have people stay on the ship as much as possible and spend their money on the ship, rather than go ashore and spend their money there. To do this, these gigantic ships provide many attractions, which is one of the reasons people take tours. Tourists want to see things and do things . . . and buy things.

Tourist Attractions

One of the reasons people take cruises is that they want to have pleasant and enriching experiences, which involves, among other things, visiting different countries and getting a sense of what these places are like. Tourists are in search of what we might call "the authentic," the real thing—whether it is a native dance on an exotic island or a visit to Ephesus in Turkey. Following are some of the attractions tourists seek:

- *Historical sites.* People want to participate in history, to be where great things happened, where history was made, so historical sites play an important role in tourism. These sites might be buildings where important events took place (e.g., the Bastille, Ground Zero in New York City) or buildings of particular interest to the tourist (for example, very old synagogues for Jewish tourists or medieval cathedrals for Christian tourists). We want to see for ourselves where history was made, so to speak. Doing so connects us, psychologically speaking, with history and with our fellow human beings.

- *Homes of the great artists, writers, scientists.* We are all curious about how great artists, writers, and scientists (and other historically important figures) lived and so visits to homes of these people offer us insights into their lives. I can recall seeing a room where Lenin had lived and was struck by how simple and austere the room was. Lenin slept on a very small and rather simple bed.
- *Museums.* On some tours we have an opportunity to visit museums where paintings or artifacts of interest are available to us. We want to see original works of great art because we all sense that doing so enriches us. Or we want to see museums with artifacts of interest. On our tour to Alaska, my wife and I visited a museum that was full of wonderful artifacts of the native tribes: totem poles, canoes, clothing, tools, cooking utensils, and so on. These artifacts offered us insights into the richness of the cultures of these peoples.
- *Natural wonders.* Tours often make it possible for people to experience many natural wonders in the world—glistening glaciers, for example, on tours to Alaska. On our cruise we visited Tracy Arms and sailed down a fjord until we were very close to an absolutely magnificent glacier. We saw small ice floes with seals. It happened to be a warm, sunny day and that trip provided what can truly be described as a transcendent experience, one that I and everyone else on the ship most likely will never forget. On cruises in the Caribbean people want to visit the various islands and go swimming at the great beaches.
- *Other cultures.* On cruises a number of stops generally enable passengers to sightsee in interesting cities and towns or arrange to have experiential tours such as taking a bus to see Ephesus in Turkey or going scuba diving in the Caribbean. People are naturally curious about the way other people live, and walking around a town or city in a foreign culture is both instructive and entertaining. Tourists like to purchase souvenirs, clothes, and other things to remind them of their experiences. Of course you only get a superficial picture of the culture you are visiting, but even that is of value. You can learn a great deal by looking; in fact, that's the way we learn most of what we know. Some passengers on our Alaskan cruise told me that they decided to take a vacation in some city or island that they first visited on a cruise.

• *Picturesque islands, beaches, and other beautiful places.* Cruise liners often stop at picturesque islands and similarly beautiful places and this kind of experience is psychologically enriching. Tourists, psychologists have found, are people who are more willing than average persons to tolerate minor risks and irritations (e.g., coping with missed flights, lost suitcases, and so on) to have enriching experiences. It is the quest for experience that is behind tourism—the quest to understand others, to see different cultures, to eat different foods, to meet different people, to have little adventures (and sometimes adventures that are not so little or not so pleasant), and to experience the beautiful.

In a sense, tourism remains the last chance most people have for adventure in life . . . the last chance to imitate the adventures of famous explorers of the past, except that on cruises, getting there is part of the fun, and the adventure is very safe and, most of the time, manicured. Cruises greatly simplify the travel experience and are useful for people who want to travel but are afraid to do so—for one reason or another—by conventional means.

Spatiality on Cruise Liners

One of the codes we learn as we grow up in the United States is that space has meaning. Our popular culture teaches us that a relationship or association exists between space and wealth. For example, the wealthy generally live in large homes with a great deal of space. It is not unusual for billionaires to have houses with 20,000 or 40,000 square feet, while ordinary, middle-class people tend to live in homes with 1,500 or 2,000 square feet. Thus, on cruise ships, generally speaking, the more space you have, the more you've paid for your cruise. This matter is complicated by whether one is in an inside cabin or an outside or "ocean-view" cabin. What an ocean-view cabin does, among other things, is enhance one's sense of the space in a cabin by connecting it visually to the sea and thus enormous vistas. The larger the ocean-view cabin, and the higher it is located on the ship, the more it costs.

The difference between private space and public space on cruise ships can also be contrasted. The private space is the cabin, which on many cruises might be 150 or 165 square feet for inside cabins that are the least expensive. The more expensive cabins are larger, but even they tend to be rather small. Outside cabins may be 180 square feet, 15 square feet larger than many inside cabins. Cabins essentially are used for people to sleep in and for little else.

The action on cruise ships is in the public or "social" spaces, which are often quite large and very impressive. On the newest megaliners these spaces are enormous. The cabins must be large enough so people don't feel too crowded or cramped, or, to use a word people thinking about taking cruises often use, "confined." But it is the public spaces that count the most.

In the cruise industry, executives use the term "space ratio," to describe the room on a ship. This figure represents the number of tons of the ship divided by the possible occupancy of the ship, assuming two people per cabin or double occupancy. A 104,000-ton ship can carry 2,600 passengers and thus has a space ratio of 40, or 4,000 cubic feet per passenger. That figure represents the amount of space on the ship per passenger. Seabourn liners are relatively small at 10,000 tons but they carry only 200 passengers, thus they have a space ratio of 50, or 5,000 cubic feet per passenger. Seabourn cruises cost approximately $800 a day per person (before discounts, that is), so people who take Seabourn cruises are paying handsomely for the added space. There are, of course, many other reasons besides having more space and maintaining social distance for why people take Seabourn cruises.

Incidentally, when cruise lines state that a ship is 100,000 tons (more precisely, gross registered tons), this is not the weight of the ship but rather the size of the ship. One gross registered ton equals 100 cubic feet of enclosed space that earns revenue—that is, the area available to passengers on the cruise—their rooms and the various public spaces.

A distinction can be made between private spaces and public or "social" spaces on cruise ships:

Private Spaces	Public Spaces
Cabins	Dining rooms, lounges, theaters, casinos, hallways, atriums, outside decks, etc.
Simple	Elegant
Functional	Impression making
Sleep and body functions	Socialization, entertainment

Actually, cabins are not completely private, since they are accessible to cabin stewards. However, these stewards are trained to clean cabins when passengers are out in public spaces and most of them are shadowy figures sometimes seen cleaning the rooms of other passengers but almost never seen cleaning our cabins.

Teak Decks and Other Luxury Signifiers

The teak deck is one of the standard signifiers of cruise ships and of luxury. These decks are generally quite beautiful and being able to walk on them and watch the sea is one of the great pleasures of cruising. Teak is used because it is very strong and resists the saltwater, but it is also a very handsome wood and sparkling clean teak decks have a richness and luminosity that cruisers find most appealing.

Other luxury signifiers are found on cruise ships, such as understated dining halls, elaborate meals, original paintings, elegant lounges, and various kinds of atriums and large public spaces. It is not unusual to have a pianist playing show tunes or pop classics in some of these spaces, much like upscale department stores, or having trios and quartets playing classical music, another indicator of cultivation and class.

Additional entertainment can be found in the elaborate shows the cruise lines offer. Some are known as "flesh and feather" spectaculars, with many beautiful young women (often in revealing costumes) and handsome young men singing and dancing, accompanied by a good-sized band and often ending with fireworks and other remarkable pyrotechnic displays. Here, the cruise lines are attempting to replicate the Las Vegas experience, except that whereas a show in Las Vegas might cost $50 or $100, on cruise ships the shows are all free.

CRUISES AND PILGRIMAGES

People have been traveling the world for thousands of years—in the interest of trade and for religious purposes, among other reasons. Until the invention of the steam engine, automobile, and airplane, most of this travel was done by sea. It's interesting to consider the difference between religious pilgrimages (and political ones, such as political conventions) and travel, in general, and cruising as a special kind of travel. Pilgrimages and travel are polar opposites in some ways, but, in a sense, they are very similar. They both involve travel for different reasons, though sometimes, religious and secular reasons overlap.

Pilgrimages	Travel
Religious	Secular
Faith	Pleasure
Superego	Id
Reinforcement	Self-Realization
Identification	Curiosity
Hardships	Comfort (especially on cruises)
Shrines	Sights

In both cases, people move around, but they are animated by different things. Pilgrims undertake travel for religious reasons, to see some famous shrine or meet a religious leader, and the purpose of this is to reinforce their identification with the religion and strengthen their attachment to it. Travelers (excluding business travel) seek pleasure and want to satisfy their curiosity about other cultures and customs. Pilgrims seek shrines that have religious significance whereas travelers seek tourist sites that have historical and cultural importance. Pilgrims are willing to put up with incredible hardships to visit holy shrines but most travelers—and this applies especially to people who take cruises—want to be comfortable and have pleasant experiences.

It can be said that travel has aspects of the pilgrimage, except that travel is generally a secularized form of the pilgrimage. Of course travelers may visit famous churches and sites that are sacred to others, but for these travelers the sights are generally of cultural, not sacred, interest. Travel, then, is an adventure and not a search for the divine.

NAMES OF CRUISE LINES AND THE PERCEIVED ELITISM OF THE CRUISE EXPERIENCE

One of the problems cruise lines face involves perceptions by the general public that cruises are for elites, upper-class snobs, "uppity" types, and so on. People don't want to pay for cruises and suffer from status anxiety. One of the core values in American culture is egalitarianism, and though passengers are no longer separated by class on cruise ships as on ocean liners of the past, people resent snobbery and situations in which they are made to feel out of place.

In 1958, I sailed to France as a third-class passenger on the French line's *Liberté*. In those days people more or less accepted that there would be different classes on ships—especially foreign ships since in European countries, class distinctions were very important. In the United States, we generally believe that we are essentially a classless nation, though some middle-class people have millions of dollars in the bank and some have very little or nothing in the bank.

The names of the cruise lines contribute to this notion that cruising is essentially an upper-class activity. Consider the names of the following cruise lines:

Celebrity
Cunard Crown Cruises
Delta Queen
Princess Cruises
Monarch
Regal
Royal Caribbean

All of these lines have words that connect them with wealth, royalty, and the aristocracy. The same applies to the names of many ships, which also have allusions to royalty. They are meant, probably, to suggest that people will have an experience worthy of royalty, but these names may discourage many people. Technically speaking, names such as Royal Caribbean and Princess Lines are signifiers of aristocracy, royalty, luxury, and perhaps snobbery—not the most desirable associations to have when trying to sell cruises to middle-class Americans with status anxieties and fears about being seasick, bored, confined, and regimented.

Many lines have names that avoid this matter of elitism and "gilt" by association such as:

Holland America
Fantasy

Dolphin
Carnival
Seabourn
Disney
Costa
Windstar
Orient
Seacliff

The names of these lines don't suggest wealth and sophistication. Image problems are exacerbated by the advertising many lines use, a topic that will be discussed in Chapter 5.

TAKING PHOTOGRAPHS AND USING VIDEO CAMERAS

Tourists take photographs for many reasons. They may want souvenirs of the places they have visited so that they can look at them again and remember, more vividly, their experiences and adventures. They may also unconsciously want to have proof that they actually visited the various places they describe to people. They also want to capture the "aura" of places—their special personalities, their beautiful sights, interesting buildings, etc.

Much of this picture taking is connected to a desire of people to participate in history, that is, to see with their own eyes the interesting and important and beautiful places found in the world and, by doing so, psychologically attach themselves to these places. A famous English writer, Matthew Arnold (1951), talked about educated people knowing "the best which has been thought and said" (p. 1119). Tourists want to see the best places that can be seen and eat the best food that can be eaten. That explains why tourist magazines often have lists of the best hotels, restaurants, and cruise lines.

The late social psychologist Stanley Milgram made an interesting point about the relationship between travel and photography in his essay "The Image Freezing Machine" (1976). He explained that taking a picture, which is similar in nature to seeing something, occurs in many situations and always involves a trade-off between passive enjoyment of a particular moment and an active process that involves taking a photograph. If you see a beautiful vista and stop to photograph it, he suggests, this means you can't fully savor your experience. In fact, he suggested that much of our travel is based on the possibility of taking photographs and that we go to beautiful places not only because they are beautiful, but also because they will make great backgrounds for our photographs. Places we visit become subordinate to their potential for beautiful pictures. Many people, he asserts, evaluate their vacations on the basis of how their pictures look.

Milgram's argument that many people travel so they can find suitable photo opportunities is worth considering. However, on the cruises I've taken, people were intent on having the best of both worlds—seeing beautiful places and taking photographs of these beautiful places, even if it meant taking a short break to take photographs. The development of video cameras and point-and-shoot cameras has made the interruptions caused by taking photos and videos less significant. In some respects, the process of taking photographs interrupts the attention tourists can give to a site—a price they seem to be willing to pay because they will have their own photographic record of the site.

CONCLUSION

For the semiotician, a semiotic analysis of a cruise is a most interesting subject. I have touched upon a number of topics that a semiotician might find interesting about the cruise phenomenon. The semiotician Peirce said "this universe is perfused with signs, if it is not composed exclusively of signs" (Sebeok, 1977, p. v). This is not necessarily true—but using the science of semiotics to analyze cruise ships and tourism is a useful way to gain valuable insights into the nature of tourism. Those interested in the semiotic analysis of tourism will find Dean MacCannell's book, *The Tourist: A New Theory of the Leisure Class* (1976) of considerable interest. He does not deal with cruising but with tourism in general. I will continue with my semiotic analysis of cruising in Chapter 5.

Cruise lines are selling you a dream. . . . The power of your dream, your imagination, creates a challenge that the cruise industry is trying to meet . . .

TV commercials and glossy color brochures about cruises all promise the same thing—an unexcelled excursion into the glamorous life, with romantic evenings, a perfect tan, six or eight gourmet meals a day, and intermittent forays into picturesque and exotic ports of call where the sun always shines, the shopping is splendid and the natives are friendly and photogenic.

Oddly enough, more often than not, it works out that way.

Shirley Slater and Harry Basch,
Fielding's Alaska Cruises

Chapter 3

Sociological Analysis of Cruising

In this chapter we consider cruising from a sociological perspective. That is, various sociological concepts will be explored to give us a better understanding of cruising. I will start with demographics. We will consider at what ages people take cruises, the income of cruisers, and matters of that nature. Sociology studies people in groups and does not focus on the discrete individual, the way psychoanalytic theory does. But like psychoanalytic theory, sociologists argue that people don't always understand the full significance of what they say and do as members of some group or organization or institution.

In *Fielding's Alaska Cruises,* Shirley Slater and Harry Basch (1997) make a number of important points. First, the image of cruising that many people have is way out of date and doesn't offer an accurate picture of what cruising is like today. In addition, the cruise industry is undergoing rapid change and evolving, in an effort to meet the many demands and high expectations of people who take cruises. Finally, they argue that cruises come through and provide highly satisfying vacations. However, there is good reason to take what they say with a grain of salt. After all, they are writing a book for people who are planning to take a cruise to Alaska, so you can assume a certain bias in terms of their view of cruising. Data from research indicate that most people who have taken cruises would agree with them. Statistics show that an overwhelming number of people who take cruises are very pleased with the experience and intend to take more cruises.

CRUISE DEMOGRAPHICS

Demographics refers to the statistical information about age, gender, ethnicity, and socioeconomic classes of people; psychographics refers to their values and beliefs, which shape much of their behavior.

In this chapter I will deal with both matters. The chart that follows is adapted from the Web site of the Cruise Lines International Association (CLIA) (see <http://www.cruising.org>), a trade organization that is charged with helping develop the cruise industry. Among other things, it offers demographic profiles of cruisers and some interesting insights into the socioeconomic status of cruisers.

	Ever Cruised	Cruised Past Five Years	Prospects	Non-Vacationers
Income				
$20,000-$29,000	8%	5%	13%	32%
$30,000-$39,000	12%	10%	17%	26%
$40,000-$59,000	32%	31%	31%	27%
$60,000-$99,000	28%	30%	29%	11%
$100,000 plus	20%	25%	9%	4%
Average (Mean)	$72,600	$79,100	$60,400	$44,200
Median	$58,000	$64,500	$51,800	$36,900
Gender				
Male	49%	51%	50%	50%
Females	51%	48%	49%	50%
Age				
25-39	27%	28%	43%	35%
40-59	42%	42%	44%	43%
60 and older	32%	30%	13%	22%
Average (Mean)	51 years	50 years	43 years	47 years
Median	51 years	51 years	42 years	47 years
Marital Status				
Married	76%	78%	69%	65%
Not Married	24%	22%	31%	35%

Education

| Some college or less | 42% | 36% | 54% | 76% |
| College grad or more | 58% | 64% | 46% | 24% |

What the Figures Reveal

One of the most interesting revelations of this chart is that cruising is essentially a middle-class or possibly upper-middle-class vacation. As Wood (2000) points out, approximately 90 percent of cruisers are from the United States. Notice that 20 percent fall in the $20,000 to $39,999 range, that approximately one-third (32 percent) of the cruises are in the $40,000 to $59,999 range, that almost one-third (28 percent) are in the $60,000 to $99,999 range, and 20 percent are in the $100,000 and above range. Approximately 60 percent of people who take cruises are college graduates while only about 25 percent of the American public has graduated from college. The average or mean family income for cruisers is approximately $72,000 (and the median is more than $58,000) which is considerably above the median household income average in the United States (as reported by the Census Bureau) of $42,228 for 2001(DeNavas-Walt and Cleveland, 2002).

A considerable difference exists between an average income (also known as the *mean* income) and a *median* income. The mean of a set of numbers is the sum of all the numbers divided by the number of numbers. For example, if you added up the incomes of everyone on a cruise and divided that number by the number of people on the cruise, you'd get the average or mean income of the passengers.

Suppose, for example, that just three families were on a cruise ship. One family had an income of $50,000, one family had an income of $60,000, and one family had an income of $100,000. The average or mean would then be found by adding the $50,000, $60,000, and $100,000 incomes, and dividing by three, which gives $70,000. The median on this cruise would be $60,000 since there are the same number of figures above it as below it.

There is a correlation between household income and cruise taking, though these figures may be misleading because we don't see how long the cruises were that people in each of these categories took. Many people take three- and four-day cruises to get a taste of what cruising is like. A short, low-end cruise can cost just a few hundred dollars, making cruises competitive with Las Vegas vacations. The cruise lines are well aware of this fact and compete with Las Vegas for vacationers looking for a good time—and perhaps the opportunity to gamble.

The age of cruisers is particularly interesting. Traditionally, we think of cruising as vacations for elderly people, but more than 25 percent of cruisers are between twenty-five and thirty-nine and 42 percent of cruisers are between forty and fifty-nine years of age. So the cruise lines have been pretty successful in attracting young and middle-aged people. These statistics may be thrown off by the increasingly large number of children who are brought along on cruises by their parents. In a room with two thirty-year-old parents and a five-year-old child, the average (mean) age of the passengers is approximately twenty-two; children can skew the statistics.

Some of the statistics are not very surprising. Approximately 50 percent of cruisers are men and 50 percent are women. That is explained by the fact that 76 percent of people who take cruises are married or are couples living together. Cruises are sold on a two-passengers-per-room basis; a single person who books a cabin must pay a high premium.

Growth by Length of Cruise—North American Market

The Cruise Lines International Association also provides data on the growth of the cruise industry in terms of the length of cruises that people take. As the chart that follows shows, reflecting shorter vacation patterns in the United States, the cruise industry's hottest growth category has been the two- to five-day cruise category, which has grown approximately twice as fast as the six- to eight-day cruise category. The following is an adaptation of a chart on the CLIA Web site (n.d.):

Cruise Popularity Over Time

	1980	2001	Growth (%)
2 to 5 days	347,000	2,566,000	639.5
6 to 8 days	846,000	3,549,000	319.5

9 to 17 days	221,000	757,000	242.5
18 + days	17,000	34,000	100.0
Totals	1,431,000	6,906,000	382.0

In 2001 2.5 million people took two- to five-day cruises and 3.5 million took six- to eight-day cruises. The two- to five-day cruises have grown the most since 1981 but a million more people took six- to eight-day cruises. Only 34,000 people took eighteen-day or longer cruises, suggesting that these cruises have very limited appeal—in part because they may be expensive and in part because most people (unless they are retired) don't have that much time to devote to cruising.

GENDER AND CRUISING

Travel, over the course of the centuries, was a pursuit of men. They went off to wars, they sailed on exploratory voyages, and they traveled on trade missions or religious pilgrimages while women, generally speaking, stayed home and looked after the children. As Eric J. Leed writes in *The Mind of the Traveler: From Gilgamesh to Global Tourism* (1991, p. 220):

> In a vast portion of human history, men have been the travelers; and travel literature is—with a few significant, and often modern exceptions—a male literature reflecting a masculine point of view. . . . The masculinization of motion and the feminization of sessility [being attached] are clearly products of cultural patterning, many examples of which occur through the travel literature. In patriarchal cultures, the mobility of men—especially of young, unattached men—is overdetermined and powerfully charged by the reigning images of masculinity, whether of the wandering knight or of the wandering holy man, the shaman or the actor.

This all changed with the modern world and the development of global tourism. We might say that cruising can be looked upon as the most "feminized" form of tourism.

All travel involves risk and dealing with unforeseen events, e.g., missed flight connections, lost baggage, trains that break down, and similar inconveniences, but cruising is the least risky and easiest form of travel. To the extent that many people define the feminine (incorrectly, I would add) in terms of the traditional stereotypes: softness, weakness, fear of risk, a love of things beautiful and cultural, and ease, the cruise, more than any other kind of tourism, can be said to be feminine. Occasionally one reads stories about crimes such as robberies and rapes taking place on ships, but generally speaking cruises are very safe.

CARNIVALIZATION THEORY AND CRUISING

Russian literary critic Mikhail Bakhtin (1984) developed a theory, commonly known as "carnivalization," that is relevant to cruising. Bakhtin's book, *Rabelais and His World,* published in Russian in 1965 and in English in 1984, explains his theory. Bakhtin's book is a study of the great writer Rabelais, author of a medieval comic work, *Gargantua and Pantagruel,* but it is much more than that, for in attempting to explain Rabelais' genius, Bakhtin tied him to the beliefs and values and celebrations of people who lived in the medieval period, and in particular to the many carnival periods that were so important to them. As Bakhtin wrote (1984, pp. 7-8):

> Carnival is not a spectacle seen by the people; they live in it, and everyone participates because its very idea embraces all the people. While carnival lasts, there is no other life outside it. During carnival time life is subject only to its laws, that is, the laws of its own freedom. It has a universal spirit; it is a special condition of the entire world, of the world's revival and renewal, in which all take part . . . carnival is the people's second life, organized on the basis of laughter. It is a festive life. Festivity is a peculiar quality of all comic rituals and spectacles of the Middle Ages.

One important aspect of carnivals was feasting. The feast, Bakhtin (1984) suggested, is an "important primary form of human culture" (p. 8). These feasts, he explained, are always related to some event in time, to important events that happened, to natural phenomena of significance. These feasts were not a form of escapism but functioned to support the status quo.

As Bakhtin writes (1984, p. 9):

> the official feasts of the Middle Ages, whether ecclesiastic, feudal, or sponsored by the state, did not lead people out of the existing world order and created no second life. On the contrary, they sanctioned the existing pattern of things and reinforced it.

That is, many feasts, especially the official ones, tended to reinforce the status quo. They did this by allowing people to escape for a short while during the carnival period from the norms of their everyday lives of hierarchy and strong class divisions. During the temporary suspensions of "the rules" of everyday life in the carnival period, people also paid no attention to the social distance between them (lord and serf, for example). They developed a speech that was intimate and liberated themselves "from norms of etiquette and decency imposed at other times" (Bakhtin, 1984, p. 10). In addition, games were an important part of carnival. These games helped people escape from the conventions that bound them during regular life, freed them from the laws that bound them, and enabled them to replace serious concerns with relatively trivial ones.

During carnival time the numerous distinctions between people, and rules and laws that existed, were suspended for a period of gaiety, licentiousness, laughter, and feasting. Cruises are a modern attempt, somewhat modified from the medieval forms of carnival, to introduce to contemporary life the sense of liberation and joy that took place during carnival time. Cruising can be seen as a sanitized and modernized form of medieval carnival. In the chart that follows lists the numerous similarities between carnival time and cruising:

Carnival Period	Cruising
particular time period	length of cruise
suspension of class differences	diminution of class differences
joyfulness and laughter	joyfulness and laughter
freedom	eat when you want, do what you want
satires and other theatrical events	shows, spectacles, comedians

feasts	eight-course meals
games	bingo, gambling, other games
abundance	twenty-four-hour dining
saturnalia	captain's champagne party
sense of community	escape from alienation

This notion is reinforced in the particular case of aptly-named Carnival cruises, for their ships are popularly understood to be "party" ships. Medieval carnivals were, Bakhtin writes, "the second life of the people, who for a time entered the utopian realm of community, freedom, equality and abundance" (1984, p. 9).

These are precisely the feelings people on cruises have or often develop—a sense of community, a sense of freedom (to eat when and where you want, to read a book, to do anything you want), a sense of equality (in that everyone, no matter whether in a lowly inside cabin or a stately suite, dines in the same dining rooms), and a sense of abundance (elaborate gourmet lunches and dinners, twenty-four-hour dining, free pizzas, and so on). On modern cruise ships, you don't find the different classes of cabins and dining rooms I experienced when I sailed third class on the French ocean liner *Liberté* between New York and Le Havre many years ago.

I can still vividly recall the sense of joy and exuberance that passengers on the *Regal Princess* felt when the ship got under way and sailed under the Golden Gate Bridge. It was a beautiful sunny day. People crowded onto the upper decks of the ship, taking photos, drinking, and enjoying the scene. A fireboat was spraying water into the bay and excitement and a sense of liberation seemed to grip everyone. It was truly a festive moment. That evening, at 5:45 p.m., at the first sitting, the feasting began.

This experience when we set sail is typical of all cruises—weather permitting, of course. This escape, if Bakhtin is correct, enables us to refresh ourselves and return to our everyday lives with what we now would describe as "recharged" batteries. Psychologists have found that vacations promote good mental health and well-being.

THE SOCIOLOGY OF DINING

This discussion draws upon the insights of the German sociologist Georg Simmel (1858-1918) who did pioneering work on the sociological aspects of many everyday life concerns, including dining with others. He pointed out that the most common or typical thing that people must do is eat and drink, and that while nobody else can eat and drink the particular portions of food that we are eating and drinking, that is, the specific items on our plates and in our glasses—typically we dine with others who eat similar foods. As he writes (quoted in David Frisby and Mike Featherstone, *Simmel on Culture* [1997, p. 130]):

> Communal eating and drinking, which can even transform a mortal enemy into a friend for the Arab, unleashes an immense socializing power that allows us to overlook that one is not eating and drinking "the same thing" at all, but rather totally exclusive portions, and gives rise to the primitive notion that one is thereby creating common flesh and blood.

This may explain the many ritual dining events in people's lives, such as at weddings, celebrations, holidays, conferences, and parties. Eating together bonds people and we derive immeasurable comfort in dining with others. At many national and religious holidays we eat special foods that unite us and at the same time separate us from those who do not partake of these dishes (such as hot dogs and hamburgers on the Fourth of July, turkeys at Thanksgiving).

Simmel points out that primitive people did not eat together at set times, but ate anarchically; whenever any individual got hungry, he or she ate something. This changed when people started sharing meals and social norms started affecting individuals. Simmel explains (Frisby and Featherstone, 1997, p. 131):

> The regulation of table manners, and their standardization according to aesthetic principles, is the result of the socialization of the meal. Among the lower classes, where the meal is essentially centered on the food in its material sense, no typical regulations regarding table manners develop. In higher social groups, in which the attraction of being together, all the way up to its—alleged, at least—culmination in "society," dominates the mere

material of the meal, a code of rules, ranging from holding the knife and fork to the appropriate subjects of table conversation, comes into being, to regulate their behavior.

He contrasts the act of dining together, with its rules and codes of etiquette, with what he calls "table d'hôte" dining, or, for our purposes, buffet lines. People at buffets gather in a room for the purpose of eating, but not for the purpose of socializing.

On cruise ships people go to the dining room and sit at tables with other people for socialization as well as eating. The buffets are much different. You may be in a large room with others but you are interested in eating rather than in socializing with others. Passengers on cruise ships may dine at the buffet precisely because they don't wish to socialize with others. In some ships, it is possible to dine at tables for two, which relieves couples of the need to socialize and converse with tablemates. Some people on cruises take "vacations" from dining in the dining room to relieve themselves of the burden of carrying on a conversation over the dinner table and the burden of choice regarding what to order from the menu.

The banality of ordinary table conversation is explained by Simmel as being a product of our need to socialize yet maintain a certain kind of distance and decorum and avoid conflicts. "Table conversation," he writes, "which should be gracious but always retain a certain generality and calmness, must never let that foundation become *completely* imperceptible, because the entire fragile lightness and grace of its surface play is revealed only when it is maintained" (Frisby and Featherstone, 1997, p. 134). Dining, in contrast to the matter of eating or ingesting food, or seeing food as a kind of fuel, has become a ritualized, stylized, and aestheticized event, and though it may seem to be trivial, in reality it reflects extremely important social matters.

On cruises, where the quality of the food is of paramount importance, other factors such as the dining room's ambiance of refinement and elegance, are also of great significance. Ship designers generally want to avoid Las Vegas-like glittery dining rooms but also those that are too austere. Interestingly enough, the success of the dining operation is tied to the design of the ship.

In *Selling the Sea,* Dickinson and Vladimir (1997) discuss this matter in some detail. They explain that deterioration of shipboard service over the years was connected to the mistakes made in designing cruise ships. Many shipboard personnel had difficulty coping with the problems created by the poor design of the ships, and this hindered them from developing good relationships with passengers and delivering the kind of service that is customarily associated with ocean cruising.

Ship architects now design cruise liners to provide quick and easy access to the kitchen areas, where food is prepared. In a sense, these architects design the ship around the galley and dining rooms. The food on most cruises can be described as excellent, quality, banquet-style cuisine; it is not cooked "à la minute" the way it is on luxury cruises such as Seabourn, but, nevertheless, the quality is quite remarkable. Ships must be designed with easy access to the galley so waiters are able to get food quickly and with as little traffic as possible. If waiters or assistant waiters are reluctant to take long trips to the galley to get something a passenger requests, there will be problems.

A distinction can be made between dining and eating on cruises:

Dining	Eating
Dining room	Buffet line
Set times	Any time
Assigned tables	Choice of seating
Elegance	Cafeteria-like ambiance
Elaborate table settings	Formica-topped tables
Menus	See what is available
Waiters	Self-serve
Sociability	Separation

This set of polarities doesn't apply as much to the new giant ships that have many different dining rooms. On these ships passengers can eat in dining rooms of their choice, more or less whenever they want, at any size tables. This gives passengers a maximum of freedom, but they lose the opportunity to get to know people at their table. Some may not mind this at all.

People taking cruises have great anxieties regarding tablemates. If tablemates are not compatible, it is often possible to move the first day, but it is an awkward matter. I know of one couple who didn't like their tablemates and switched tables three times before ending up at a table for two for the remainder of their cruise.

The army, it is said, travels on its stomach. So do passengers on cruise ships.

TIME BUDGETS AND THE BUSY LIFE AT SEA

Passengers who like to eat in the dining room can eat breakfast, lunch, and dinner there. They can also enjoy midafternoon tea, when white-gloved waiters serve small sandwiches, pastries, scones, and other delicacies. A talkative person can easily spend an hour having breakfast, an hour having lunch, an hour at tea, and two hours having dinner, adding up to approximately five hours in the dining room. (On some cruises, afternoon tea isn't served in the dining room; it wasn't in the dining room every afternoon on the *Regal Princess,* being served elsewhere some days.)

During the cruise to Alaska on the *Regal Princess,* I often spent five hours a day in the dining room. In between my various meals I read, walked around the cities where the ship stopped (sometimes on three- or four-hour excursions), went to shows, wandered around the ship, went dancing with my wife, attended lectures, and listened to music, among other things. Before we took the cruise my wife wondered whether she'd be bored. We had been bored at times on our seven-day cruise to Puerto Vallarta, having been reduced to taking a class in napkin folding. We were facing a ten-night cruise to Alaska.

But our experience on the *Regal Princess* was quite different from our cruise to Puerto Vallarta; we were also on a larger ship with more facilities. What follows is a list of some of the activities available on a typical "at sea" day when the *Regal Princess* wasn't calling at any port. This list shows the large variety of activities on a cruise ship; the larger cruise ships probably have even more activities. This list, which is somewhat of a composite, is taken from the *Princess Patter: A Daily Guide to Cruise Activities,* which was delivered to our cabin every evening.

8:00 a.m. Step Xpress class
9:00 a.m. Pathway to Yoga class ($10)
9:15 a.m. Port and shopping talk on Juneau and Ketchikan
9:30 a.m. Bridge players lecture

9:45 a.m. Mixed-doubles shuffleboard
9:45 a.m. Poker players meet in card room
10:00 a.m. Mahjong players get-together
10:00 a.m. Masonic get-together
10:15 a.m. Wildlife presentation by on-board naturalist
11:00 a.m. Lotus Spa seminar. De-Tox for Weight Loss
11:15 a.m. Bingo
11:15 a.m. Quiz-lovers game
11:30 a.m. Needlepoint class
1:30 p.m. Golf-putting tournament
2:00 p.m. Duplicate and party bridge
2:15 p.m. Backgammon players get-together
2:15 p.m. Line-dance class
2:30 p.m. Art auction
2:30 p.m. Movie (also 5:00, 8:00 and 10:00 p.m.)
3:00 p.m. Wine-tasting seminar ($5)
3:30 p.m. Afternoon tea, with music of Melodic Trio
3:45 p.m. Police and firefighters get-together
4:00 p.m. Chess players get-together
4:00 p.m. Kickbox Xpress class ($10)
4:00 p.m. Ping-Pong warm-up for tournament
4:15 p.m. Bingo
4:15 p.m. Quiz time
4:15 p.m. Scavenger hunt
5:00 p.m. Cocktail karaoke sing-along
5:00 p.m. Honeymooners get-together
5:00 p.m. Friends of Dr. Bob and Bill W. (Alcoholics Anonymous)
5:00 p.m. Lotus Fusion class
5:45 p.m. First seating for dinner
7:15 p.m. Dance party in Stage Door
8:00 p.m. Show with singers, dancers, orchestra (also 9:45 p.m.)
8:45 p.m. Dance party in Adagio lounge
8:45 p.m. Second seating for dinner
9:00 p.m. Dance party in Dome
9:30 p.m. Name that tune
11:00 p.m. Dance party in Stage Door

Numerous activities were available throughout the day for those who wanted to keep busy, and I didn't list every event on that day. Those who might want to read or just relax, could do that as well. Passengers could also watch others who were taking dancing classes, playing in tournaments, gambling, or dancing. On our cruise we ended up leaving wake-up calls for 7:30 a.m. so my wife (sometimes joined by me) could work out in the gym and so we could participate in the various things we wanted to do. Unlike everyday life, on cruises just about everything one does or can do is connected with pleasure and entertainment.

The schedule is cleverly designed to lure people who dine at the first sitting out of the dining room, so that they can get good seats for the evening shows and the dining room staff can get ready for the second sitting at 8:45 p.m. Thus, most evenings my wife and I left the dining room around 7:45 p.m. and went to the theater to see the Vegas-style shows—some of which were quite spectacular.

NEW TRENDS IN CRUISING

Cruising, like anything else, is affected by social change and the nature of the travel market. In order to broaden its base, the cruise industry has made considerable changes. New trends in the cruise industry are a response to research, mentioned earlier, which indicates that people who are not dedicated cruisers are anxious about four perceived problems:

1. fear of seasickness,
2. fear of boredom,
3. fear of regimentation, and
4. fear of confinement and being "out of contact" with family and friends.

One can combat boredom by scheduling different activities throughout the day. You *can* be bored on a cruise ship but you have to work at it!

The fear of regimentation is a different matter. Most of this anxiety stems from being *assigned* to specific tables with strangers and to first or second sittings—on ships that have two sittings, that is. To counter this problem, the new cruise ships have done away with assigned tables and now passengers can dine in any one of a number of different dining venues. Schedules on older vessels allow people to dine whenever they wish at twenty-four-hour buffets or similar kinds of arrangements.

Cruise ships are, as Dickinson and Vladimir (1997) explain, paramilitary organizations in which rules, rank, and discipline are very important. This can create problems, since cruise lines are service industries that depend upon customer satisfaction for their success. The hierarchical nature of a ship's staff, with a powerful captain and a number of rules that must be obeyed, goes against the grain of most Americans, who have an egalitarian value system and chafe at rules and regulations or anyone telling them what to do, especially on vacation.

The authoritarian aspect of the captain's position and the officers is mitigated by having the captain, and to some degree other officers, socialize with passengers. He poses with passengers for pictures, he throws a champagne party with free champagne, he mingles at parties. Thus, the rather rigid nature of the command structure of the ship is kept out of sight. The captain's presence in social settings may be comforting to passengers who are anxious about being at sea and worry about the ship sinking during rough seas. The captain assures people that smooth sailing will occur during the cruise.

Anxiety about confinement concerns being stuck in a small cabin and being out of communication with friends and family. Today, many cruise ships have Internet cafes as well as satellite phone-call arrangements, but they are fairly expensive. However, since a large percentage of people on cruises now have cell phones, they can easily keep in touch with people at the various ports the cruise ships call on. Pay phones are available for passengers who don't have cell phones.

Another important trend in the cruise industry involves the building of gigantic cruise liners, some of which are 110,000 tons, twenty stories high, and can accommodate 3,000 passengers. Some large liners have ten- or fifteen-story atriums, shopping malls, and ice-skating rinks. These ships are designed with almost all rooms being sea view (or atrium view). Many have private balconies and are incredibly luxurious.

CONCLUSION

A short while after I returned from my cruise to Alaska, I got into a conversation with a neighbor, who asked me about my cruise. He informed me that he and his wife were in Alaska about the same time we were, but that they flew to Alaska, rented cars to get around (where driving between cities was possible), took ferries, and stayed in bed-and-breakfasts.

"The proprietors of bed-and-breakfasts have lots of jokes about people who take cruises," he said, chuckling to himself. He was asserting that his trip in Alaska was, somehow, more "authentic" than mine because he avoided "luxury" cruisers and he could stay for as long as he wanted in towns such as Juneau and Sitka. My thought was that Juneau and Sitka, lovely as they are, were only worth a few hours or so and that he probably equated being uncomfortable and having to make all kinds of complicated travel arrangements with authenticity.

In an article titled "If It's Tuesday . . .," Bob Knotts (2002), a travel writer, describes a cruise he took. He reassessed his skepticism about the ship's itinerary when his ship sailed along the shoreline in Norway through the many islands in the Swedish archipelago on the way to Stockholm. He was able to observe nature and the towns in these countries close-up and in some cases see people who were boating who waved to the passengers on his ship. He believed this gave him a personal connection with the people in these countries.

He describes how his wife and he were able to accomplish judicious sightseeing at each port stop, wandering around and interacting with local people. They visited the important sites in all the cities they stopped at during the time they had ashore, generally around eight hours.

He concludes:

> By now, of course, I had answered my own question: Can visiting ten countries over 15 days by cruise ship offer any worthwhile travel experience? It can, I discovered—a traveler's eagerness to seek out the worth is all that's needed. (Knotts, 2002, p. 123)

Knotts makes an important point: cruise ships provide travelers who wish to do so with the opportunity to see a great deal and to have authentic and memorable experiences.

On a ship, dining room utilization and consumer demand are predictable and controlled even to the point of knowing exactly what percentage of guests will opt for Veal Milanese at the Captain's dinner or Escargot on French night. As a result, at any comparable price point, cruise ships can deliver a food product superior to that of their land-based competitors.

But it gets even better than that. Because of precise predictability, very high utilization of food (which translates into almost no spoilage), and very fresh foodstuffs, almost any cruise can offer a better dining experience at a much lower cost, thus contributing meaningfully to the value advantage of cruising as a vacation.

The cruise industry looks at food costs on a per-diem or per passenger-day basis. In the ultra-luxury end of the market, it is not uncommon to spend $25 to $30 (per passenger 24 hour day) for the raw food (exclusive of labor and overhead). In the premium segment, the cost is typically in the neighborhood of $8-18, and for mass-market, costs run $8 to 11. Passengers can have (and some do have) one breakfast in the cabin, another one on deck, and a third in the dining room. And that's not all. They can eat lunch twice—on deck and in the dining room—and have an eight-course dinner! Of course, there are also mid-morning and mid-afternoon snacks to tide you over, as well as one or two late-night buffets. If that's not enough, if you're still hungry . . . there's twenty-four hour room service on most ships; and . . . many pizza parlors and ice cream bars are open much of the day (pp. 52, 53).

Bob Dickinson and Andy Vladimir,
Selling the Sea: An Inside Look at the Cruise Industry

Chapter 4

A Psychoanalytic Interpretation of Cruising

In this chapter psychoanalytic theory will be used to interpret various aspects of cruising—an exercise that has led to some interesting, surprising, and perhaps "far-out" notions. Two situations are possible: ocean cruising has some hidden aspects that are truly remarkable when revealed, or I have gone off the deep end, so to speak, and read all kinds of things into cruising, coming up with conclusions that are far-fetched and ridiculous. Keep an open mind and consider whether any of the analogies and interpretations might be true. (As I used to tell my students who accused me of being "far out," I'm in the center and you are all "far in!")

Although approximately only 12 or 13 percent of the American public has taken cruises, a high percentage of cruisers have taken many cruises. On my *Regal Princess* cruise, I met a couple who had taken twenty-five cruises and a travel agent told me that she knew of someone who had taken one hundred cruises. These may be rather extreme cases, but many people on cruises are on their tenth or fifteenth cruise.

THE COMPULSION TO CRUISE

Why do people (often elderly couples but not always) take so many cruises? Is there an element of what is known in psychoanalytic theory as "repetition compulsion" involved in this kind of behavior? Repetition compulsion generally involves the need to repeat certain experiences as a means of trying to deal with certain traumas, generally experienced in childhood. This process is unconscious and perfectly normal, except in extreme cases. On the conscious level, people take cruises to repeat pleasurable experiences of previous cruises. But the conscious decision to take cruises may be connected with the unconscious desire, or perhaps even the need, to take them. (We might ask the same question of people who like to travel who are compulsive travelers, except that travel doesn't supply the gratifications found on cruises as easily or quite the same way that cruising does.)

In *Selling the Sea,* Dickinson and Vladimir interviewed a couple who had been on forty cruises, averaging one cruise every two months. The couple described themselves as addicted to cruising. They had traveled 40,000 miles on Holland America ships and to celebrate that achievement, Holland America lines gave them a special emblem. What this couple called an addiction can be described as a repetition compulsion.

To understand this phenomenon—the fact that some people take many cruises—consider the psychological gratifications that cruises offer people and the uses people make of the cruising experience. That is, cruises have certain functions for cruisers that lead them to repeat the cruise experience.

Cruises offer distractions and diversions, that is, escape from the worries and anxieties that are part of normal, day-to-day existence. Cruises are now designed to provide activities for people from morning to evening. It is easy to become immersed in activities and forget about troubles. Aside from the ship's newspaper, which generally only lists events going on in the ship, and cable television news available on the television set in your cabin, you are pretty well cut off from the world.

Another gratification involves experiencing the beautiful, which involves everything from the physical beauty of cruise ships to the gorgeous seascapes and the spectacular island paradises many cruise ships visit. The elegance of the dining experience suggests to cruisers that they are leading "the good life." These stolen moments of luxury and refinement generally are a temporary but very pleasant interlude from ordinary life.

Most people, for example, do not eat six-course dinners when they are dining at home. Cruises also enable us to be with people, to take care of our need to socialize. We are, after all, social animals. Cruises provide excellent real-life (as contrasted with televised or film) entertainment, with shows, singers, comedians, magicians, and musicians available a good deal of the time. Cruise ships also have movie theaters.

Thus, these positive reinforcements on cruises lead to a mild form of compulsion in most people, and, for some, a very powerful "need" to be on cruises. Cruising has an unconscious but powerful emotional impact on people and the cruise experience functions somewhat like a drug that provides pleasurable inputs to the brain, which perhaps, leads some people to become "hooked" on taking cruises. It is possible that cruising provides pleasures, which become cravings, that can only be satisfied by repeating the cruising experience. Repetitive cruising is a mild form of compulsion that is not psychologically harmful, though it does considerable damage to one's bank account and, in many cases, waistline.

SEA AND PSYCHE

Many people exhibit anxiety about being at sea and suffering from seasickness. This is one of the main problems cruise companies face. The other side of this coin is that people who go to sea can then feel a mild sense of accomplishment about taking a cruise and being at sea. On most cruises, the sea presents no problem, but nevertheless represents a source of anxiety for large numbers of people. This feeling of accomplishment, of having braved the sea, is probably unconscious, but it still exists.

The sea fascinates people. It has a life of its own, and under the waves live all kinds of incredible creatures, such as dolphins and whales, that occasionally show themselves. On the cruises I've taken, passengers become very excited when whales are sighted and make a mad rush to the side of the boat where the whales can be seen. People are also fascinated by the power of the sea—by the waves that come crashing against the ships when the seas are rough, by the emptiness on the surface, beneath which a savage battle for survival takes place among the creatures of the sea—fish, squid, sharks, sea snakes, octopuses, turtles, seals.

This metaphor of a relatively quiet surface and turmoil underneath is one that psychoanalytic theorists have used to deal with the unconscious. I have used another metaphor, that of an iceberg. The part of the iceberg we see represents consciousness; the area of the iceberg a few feet beneath the sea, which can be seen and thus is accessible to people, represents preconsciousness; and the black area beneath this layer of a few feet or so, an area that cannot be seen and is not accessible to us under ordinary circumstances, represents the unconscious. Freudian psychoanalytic theory argues that the unconscious often shapes and determines how people behave—that is, their unconscious shapes their consciousness in the same way that currents and eddies under the sea affect the surface of the sea.

According to Freud, many human actions are connected to unconscious imperatives in our psyches. We rationalize a lot of our behavior, devising good reasons to explain what we've done, but in reality other forces, of which we are unaware, determine our actions. As Ernest Dichter, the "father" of motivation research, wrote in his book *The Strategy of Desire* (2002, p. 12), "Whatever your attitude toward modern psychology or psychoanalysis, it has been proved beyond any doubt that many of our daily decisions are governed by motivations over which we have no control and of which we are often quite unaware."

The noted psychologist Carl G. Jung added some insights that are of interest here. As he explains in *Man and His Symbols* (1968, p. 20):

> We all see, hear, smell, and taste many things without noticing them at all at the time, either because our attention is deflected or because the stimulus to our senses is too slight to leave a conscious impression. The unconscious, however, has taken note of them, and such subliminal sense perceptions play a significant part in our everyday lives. Without our realizing it, they influence the way in which we react to both events and people.

Jung's point, that our unconscious is affected by things that we don't pay any conscious attention to, is very important because it suggests why there can be an unconscious component to our psyches. He adds another relevant point (1968, p. 22):

> Many people overestimate the role of will power and think that nothing can happen to their minds that they do not decide and intend. But one must learn to discriminate carefully between intentional and unintentional contents of the mind. The former are derived from the ego personality; the latter, however, arise from a source that is not identical with its "other side."

The arguments made by Freud, Dichter, and Jung describe the unconscious, explain why its contents are not accessible to us, point out that there are "unintentional" contents to the unconscious, and suggest that our unconscious affects many decisions we make. That is, we do not and cannot understand the significance of many of the things we do—which can be traced back to the unconscious elements in our psyches.

Another analogy may be relevant to understanding some unconscious aspects of cruising. Consider a fetus in its mother's womb, surrounded and nourished by amniotic fluid. It is possible that the cruise represents something vaguely similar and that the cruise experience parallels or can be seen as analogous to being back in the womb. In the womb, all needs are taken care of; that paradise is disturbed by being born, or in the case of cruising, having to disembark. All of this exists at the unconscious level, of course.

This may strike some people as very far-fetched, and yet I think a case can be made for the analogy. Consider that many people avoid cruises because they don't want to be confined to a little cabin and locked into being on a ship where it is impossible to get in your car and drive away for a change of scenery.

THE PARADISE MYTH AND CRUISES

The story of Adam and Eve is relevant to the cruise experience because cruise ships are seen as paradisical (that is, as places very much like the Garden of Eden). This explains our feelings of exultation when we get on a cruise ship and our feelings of sadness when we leave one. Let me quote some passages from Genesis:

> And God said, "Let us make man in our image, after our likeness: and let them have dominion over the fish of the sea, and over the fowl of the air, and over the cattle, and over all the earth, and over every creeping thing that creepeth upon the earth." So God created man in his own image, in the image of God created he him; male and female created he them.

> And the Lord God planted a garden eastward in Eden; and there he put the man whom he had formed. And out of the ground made the Lord God to grow every tree that is pleasant to the sight, and good for food; the tree of life also in the midst of the garden, and the tree of knowledge of good and evil. . . . And the Lord God commanded the man saying "Of every tree of the garden thou mayest freely eat: but of the tree of the knowledge of good and evil though shalt not eat of it: for the day that thou eatest of it therefore thou shalt surely die." (*The Bible Designed to Be Read As Living Literature*, 1951, pp. 4-6)

The rest of the story is well-known. God created Eve out of one of Adam's ribs. The snake in the Garden of Eden persuaded Eve to eat from the tree of the knowledge of good and evil and she then persuaded Adam to eat from the tree. When God discovered that they had done this, he threw them both out of the Garden of Eden. From that period on, man had to live by the sweat of his brow, woman would bear children in sorrow, and snakes had to crawl on their stomachs. A short while after the story of the Garden of Eden, we read about Noah and his ark, which also has relevance to the matter of being at sea.

On cruises, pleasant sights and good food abound. This food doesn't cost anything when we eat it so cruises project a paradisical, Eden-like quality. On cruises people don't use real money; instead, everything is paid for by a plastic card. Psychologically, money is dirty (which explains the term "filthy lucre") but plastic is clean and doesn't have the associations of actual money). Since we are cut off from the problems of the real world—even if only temporarily—by being at sea, we exist in a state of relative innocence. On cruises the snake in the Garden of Eden is represented by the waiters who urge us to eat the desserts that are available to us (but eating rich desserts is a relatively minor sin [gluttony] in the scheme of things). In the following chart I compare our lives in the Garden of Eden and the cruising experience.

An unconsciously or only dimly recognized paradisical element exists to cruising, even though we may not think of cruises in such terms. A number of parallels are found between the biblical story of Adam and Eve and Noah's ark and the cruise experience.

Garden of Eden	Cruises
pleasant sights	beautiful ship and gorgeous vistas
freely eat	free food in abundance
no knowledge of good and evil	lack of news about world
snake	waiters and rich desserts they bring
thrown out for tasting tree	debarking after cruise
Noah's ark	cruise ship
forty days on ark	long cruise

CRUISE LINERS AS FLOATING UTOPIAS

In a similar vein, we can see cruise liners as temporary (for the duration of the cruise) utopian societies, which take care of all needs and are highly organized and efficient. The term "utopia" literally means no place (from the Greek *ou*: not, no + *topas*: place). Utopian communities have been set up in the United States over the years, especially in the nineteenth century. Typically, they were led by charismatic individuals who determined what everyone did in the community; among the better aspects of this leadership position was a choice of sleeping companions. The utopian communities either collapsed due to internal disputes or faded away when their charismatic leaders died.

Utopias are attempts to achieve paradise on Earth by setting up communities where everyone is treated equally, where social pathology and social strife is eliminated, and people can find ways to actualize themselves. To do this, these communities needed some kind of structure to keep everything going.

Cruise ships, with their highly structured organization—from the captain, as the highest authority, with other levels of command beneath him or her, down to the dishwashers and brass polishers—have characteristics similar to utopian communities. There is law and order, there is structure, there is no want. Indeed, for passengers who buy into this utopian community both literally and figuratively, all needs are resolved. Stewards look after the cabins, leaving little chocolates in the evening, and waiters and their assistants take care of serving passengers food, which is always available. Similar to the utopian communities of the past, those who are more or less hidden away do most of the work and are paid very little for their labors, as a rule.

HEDONISM AND PLEASURE SEEKING

The cruise experience must be seen against the context of American culture because Americans take 90 percent of all cruises. Statistics indicate that Americans tend to work longer hours and have less vacation time than people from countries such as France or Germany. Many German workers get six weeks of vacation (six weeks is the norm for Europe now), which contrasts with the two or three weeks of the typical American worker. America has strong elements of anhedonism in it, that is, a lack of hedonism and little concern for pleasure . . . or, perhaps, little opportunity to have pleasure. Some statistics are relevant:

- 16 percent of workers in the United States are too busy to take off all the vacation days that are due to them.
- 20 percent of workers in the United States claim they never take vacations.
- 13 days of vacation per year is the average for workers in the United States.
- 42 days of vacation per year is the average for workers in Italy.
- 33 percent of workers in the United States check in with their bosses during vacations.
- 40 percent of workers in the United States skip vacations due to tighter budgets and increased workloads.

This may explain why Americans who take cruises have been described by Australian scholar Jim Macbeth as deviants—people who are different from the typical anhedonic American. That is, cruise-taking Americans are in search of pleasure and find cruises to be highly pleasurable experiences. A large number of cruisers are retired, and thus have two important characteristics: they have ample time and they have enough money to take many cruises.

CRUISE TAKING AS REGRESSION
IN THE SERVICE OF THE EGO

Cruise taking is a kind of regression. Regression is an unconscious action that people resort to as a means of strengthening their egos and helping them resist the attacks of their superegos. This behavior is perfectly normal and not connected with neurosis. Freud suggested that the human psyche is divided into three parts: an id, ego, and superego. The id, our drives, seeks pleasure and gives people energy; the ego, which focuses on our relation to the outside world, tries to balance the id and superego forces in our psyches; the superego, or conscience, is always telling us to act morally and avoid temptation. If our ids are too strong, we can't concentrate on anything and we dissipate our energies; if our superegos are too strong, we are so guilt ridden that we can't do much.

The ego seeks ways to balance these two forces with defense mechanisms. One of the methods it uses is regression, which involves a return to earlier stages of development when life was simpler and we experienced unconditional love. In everyday life, for example, eating an ice cream cone has regressive aspects to it; we return to our younger days when eating ice cream was a supreme pleasure. Interestingly enough, ice cream was always available for desserts on the dinner menu on our cruise.

The size of these ships also supports the regression hypothesis. On giant ships we are all so small, relatively speaking, that, psychologically speaking, we take on a childlike semblance. In addition, we know that mysterious things are occurring in parts of the ship that are off limits to passengers. The most we get to do is visit the galley and the bridge, but we don't get to visit the engine room or other places where all those "crew only" signs are found.

Freud argued that individuals pass through certain stages as they mature. They start at the *oral* stage (the baby sucking a pacifier because it wants to suck), move on to the *anal* stage, then to the *phallic* stage, and finally end up at the *genital* stage. On cruises, food plays a major role in the scheme of things and it can be argued that we temporarily regress to the oral stage for a considerable time while cruising. We are not conscious of this or that the cruise liner facilitates our returning to this oral stage by having such lavish meals, but it seems quite evident that the quality of the food is a major consideration for cruise takers. Following is the menu for a French dinner on Princess lines. It is very similar to menus offered by all cruise lines for their French dinners.

Hors d'oeuvres
Escargots Bourguignon
Symphonie de Fruits Royales
Mixed Fresh Fruits Marinated with Fine Champagne and Kirsch and Served with a Raspberry Coulis
Pâté de Foile de Strasbourg
Liver Pâté Strasbourg Style with Black Truffles, Garnished with Aspic, Flavored with Vintage Port Wine, and Warm Toast Points

Soups
Soupe a L'oignon Gratinée
Velouté Petit Jean
Puree of Pumpkins and Turnips, Garnished with a Chiffonade of Lettuce, Basil, Cream, and Butter
Chilled Vichyssoise

Salad
Mixed Greens and Radicchio with choice of French, Walnut Vinaigrette, or Low-Fat Ranch Dressing

Princess Favorites
Nouilles Fagon Cannebiere
Egg Fettuccine Simmered in a Light Creamy Lobster Sauce

Entrées
Saumon au Fenouil (Salmon Filet Sautéed with Olive Oil, Served with a Fennel Pernod Sauce)
Coquilles St. Jacques Nicoise (Scallops Served on a Bed of Tomatoes, Eggplant, Zucchini, Black Olives, and Fresh Herbs)
Canard aux Cabernet Cassis Sauce (Roasted Slices of Long Island Duckling Breast in a Cabernet Wine Sauce, Presented with Braised Red Cabbage, Tomatoes Provençal, and Macaire Potatoes)

Pork Normand (Roast Center Cut of Pork Loin Flambéed with
   Calvados and Garnished with Baked Granny Smith Apples)
Entrecôte au Poivre Vert (Grilled Steak, Flambéed with Cognac
   and Served with a Pepper Sauce)

Always Available
Classic Caesar Salad
Broiled Atlantic Silver Salmon Filet
Grilled Skinless Chicken Breast
Grilled Black Angus Sirloin Steak
Baked Potato and French Fries can be requested in addition to
   the daily vegetable selection

Desserts
Flambéed Bing Cherries Jubilee à la mode
Raspberry Crème Brûlée
Apple Tart Tatin
Caramelized Apple Tart Baked Upside Down

From the Ship's Ice Cream Fountain
Lime Sherbet
Hazelnut Glacé
Vanilla Fudge Glacé

Assorted International and French Cheeses, with Crackers
St. Paulin
Roquefort
Camembert

On the cruise I took I spent a lot of time in the elegant dining room
of the ship, where there were always starched napkins, where waiters
were always filling water glasses with ice water, and where waiters
seized your napkin and unfolded it on your lap, if you weren't fast
enough to grab it yourself. On the last cruise I took on the *Regal Princess* (a ten-day cruise from San Francisco to Alaska and back) I spent
about five hours in the dining room each day. This worked out as follows:

Breakfast—one hour (or more when I accompanied my wife to
the buffet)
Lunch—one hour plus
Tea—one hour
Dinner—two hours

During the meals I spent a good deal of time chatting with people we
met at the open seatings for breakfast, lunch, and tea. Nevertheless, I
spent a considerable amount of time dining, and I don't imagine I was
that different from many other people on the cruise.

I happened to prefer the dining hall to the buffet on the tenth floor
of the ship, which I felt was more like a cafeteria and wasn't as much
fun for me. There were several days when my wife slept late and went
to the buffet for breakfast. I joined her, so she wouldn't have to eat
alone, and that added time to my list. What I did those days was eat
half of my breakfast in the dining room and the other half of my
breakfast in the buffet area of the ship. I liked having breakfast in the
dining room because I thought the food was better, but also because I
could get delicious cappuccinos from the ship's espresso machine.

The point is, dining is one of the most important activities—and
selling points—for cruise lines. People who take cruises want to dine
well and generally they do, though cooking dinner for 800 people per
sitting and giving people what they want takes some doing. I found
the quality of the food remarkable. The food on most cruise ships
may be banquet-style food, but because the quality of the cooking is
so good and because there are so many choices, people tend to think
of the meals they eat in the dining room as "gourmet." Cruise lines
also have identical menus, and all their ships serve the same meals on
a given day, which makes things a great deal easier on everyone involved with food preparation.

This high quality was possible because the *Regal Princess* has a
huge staff of cooks and others in the food service: an executive chef,
three sous chefs, ten first chefs, twelve second chefs, eleven third
chefs, five bakers, a maître d'hôtel, six headwaiters, forty-eight waiters, forty-seven junior waiters, an assistant maître d'hôtel, a buffet supervisor, and twenty-four buffet stewards. In addition, there was also
a galley supervisor, nineteen dishwashers, four pan cleaners, four
galley cleaners, a chief butcher and five helpers, a provision master
and five helpers, a pantry master and five helpers, an ice carver, and

so on—for a total of 266 food and beverage employees. That comes to around one food and beverage employee for every six passengers on the ship.

THE GOURMET/GOURMAND PROBLEM

A gourmet is someone who likes fine food. A gourmand is a glutton. Where do you draw the line? The answer is easy:

I am a gourmet, we tell ourselves;
YOU are a lover of fine food, we tell our friends and acquaintances;
HE or SHE is a glutton, we say about others.

The cruise director often joked, "People come on as passengers and leave as cargo," adding that it wasn't unusual for people to gain five pounds during a cruise. That would mean a typical passenger would, on average, gain a half a pound each day—quite an incredible accomplishment and a most undesirable one, also. This is more weight gain on a daily basis than steers at a feedlot.

On cruises food is readily accessible and this temptation is very strong for compulsive eaters. In the United States, approximately 33 percent of the population is obese, due to the kinds and quantities of food consumed. For these people, a cruise represents an opportunity to eat continually and obsessively. I noticed a considerable number of very obese people on the Princess cruise. Whether the cruise was paradise or hell for them is unknown.

Interestingly enough, and to her great delight, my wife lost two pounds on the *Regal Princess* cruise—in part because of all the exercise we had and in part because she avoided rich desserts. In fact, it is possible to eat the six-course dinners and not gain weight if one is careful about what one orders and avoids rich desserts. I didn't gain any weight, in part because I usually avoided the rich desserts and in part because I did so much walking on the ship and when we docked.

The dining room had various theme dinners. Following is a list of foods I ate at the farewell dinner:

Shrimp Cocktail
Chilled Cream of Hawaiian Papaya and Banana Soup

Salad with Olive Oil and Balsamic Vinegar
Linguine alla Scarpara
King Crab Legs with Melted Butter . . . New Red Potatoes
Baked Alaska on Parade
Cheese Platter
Decaffeinated Cappuccino

It took a long time to eat this meal and it was one of the more calorific meals I had while on board, especially since the waiter gave me a huge portion of the baked Alaska and dribbled a large amount of chocolate syrup on it.

UNCONDITIONAL LOVE

When we are babies and very young children, before our parents start making demands of us, we experience unconditional love. We are loved just for being who we are. Later, when we get older, this unconditional love is often withdrawn and love becomes conditional, a reward for doing things our parents want us to do. On cruise ships, especially in the dining hall, we all experience unconditional love again.

The waiters are always smiling, always attentive to our needs, and they are pleased to get us anything on the menu we might want. Once during lunch I ordered a dish that included spinach and someone at my table saw the spinach and thought it looked good, so he asked the waiter if he could have a side of spinach. "Of course," said the waiter. Two minutes later, he slid a plate of spinach onto the table next to the man. The point is, you can have anything you want, and if you don't like something, you don't have to eat it and can get something else. The waiters are very polite and very unobtrusive, and they exist to satisfy your every desire. They are, then, like ideal substitute parents who offer us unconditional love—through food.

THE AGONY OF THE CHOICE

Once, after having an appetizer and a soup, I ordered tempura for my main course. A passenger who was sitting opposite me had ordered a sandwich, but I noticed him looking enviously at my tempura.

"How's your sandwich?" I asked.

"Excellent," he replied. "But I think I made a mistake. I was originally planning on ordering the tempura but I was afraid it would be too greasy, so I ordered the sandwich."

"It's not greasy at all," I replied. "It is really wonderful . . . with juicy shrimp and very delicately fried vegetables. I'm surprised at how good it is. Why don't you order it? You don't have to finish your sandwich."

"No," he replied. "As long as I have the sandwich, I'll eat it. But I made a mistake."

"Indeed you did," I said, rubbing it in with glee. The man had been raised during the years when mothers told their children, "finish your meal . . . children in Europe are starving" and felt that not finishing his sandwich would be morally reprehensible.

"You don't know what you're missing!" I told him.

Every meal on a cruise ship forces people into what might be called "the agony of choice." These choices are trivial in the scheme of things—yet people want to maximize their dining experience and order the best food, especially since it doesn't cost them anything out of pocket. (We actually pay for our food up front, when we buy our tickets, but the food doesn't *seem* to cost anything when we eat.) So we feel a bit guilty about not having ordered correctly, even if what we ordered was good . . . but not as good, we think, as what someone else at our table ordered. I generally relied on our waiter's suggestions after asking his opinion of the menu choices. Most of the time he was correct.

The food service personnel know from experience that certain dishes will be favored by most diners and are thus able to plan how much of any food they should cook. For example, during the French dinner everyone at my table ordered the escargot and many also ordered the onion soup. It is true that we can eat whatever we want from the menu, but in reality most of us are predisposed to order certain dishes and making choices isn't always as agonizing as it might seem to be.

Most of us are predisposed toward certain "high status" foods. One evening when king crab legs were being served, it seemed as if everyone in the dining room had ordered them; the same applied to lobster tails. Forecasting is very precise and important, since the cooks must have the right amount of each kind of food on hand for the cruise.

Whenever I passed by the doorway to the dining hall, people were looking at the menu for the next meal, trying to figure out their best choice. This agony of choice isn't as strong at the buffet line, where people can see everything that is available and take whatever they want. Some prefer the buffet precisely because it spares them from the agony of choice.

ESCAPING THE BOREDOM OF EVERYDAY LIFE

Most people's lives are very routine and boring. Thoreau said that most men lead lives of "quiet desperation." Actually, some boredom isn't so bad; we are not designed for constant challenge and excitement and find comfort in the steady quality of our everyday lives. Yet, we also like to escape from our routines (and ourselves) from time to time. This explains why we go to the movies, to shows, the theater, to museums, to the symphony, and to the ballet. These activities provide moments of escape and enrichment for us. In books, films, and the theater, we escape into other people's lives and gain insights about the meaning of life. In museums and the symphony and the ballet, we search for beauty. These escapes enrich us and make us able to better tolerate our everyday routines.

Cruising can be seen as an escape attempt—a means of breaking out of the ruts we are in and the routines that dominate our lives. Cruises provide a short period of intense and extremely rich experiences—excellent food, music, lectures, dancing, live shows, and different places to visit. Just as bears store up fat for their winter hibernation, cruise takers store up fun and pleasant experiences thus providing comforting memories during their everyday lives.

For weeks after our cruise was over, my wife and I talked about it, certain meals we had, about our waiter and assistant waiter, about the places we visited, about people we met, and about the shows we saw. Some nights I even dreamed I was back on the cruise . . . wandering around the ship, watching people playing bingo, taking dance lessons, gambling in the casino, or being faced with a gigantic slice of baked Alaska.

BEHIND THE FACADE:
DAILY LIFE OF CREW MEMBERS

I often wondered about what our waiters and our steward *really* thought about us and all the other people with whom they dealt. They always projected the smile—the front that they had been taught to put on. But what was behind that front? Of course, it is possible that they were so busy and dealt with so many people during the year that we all became ciphers for them. Possibly, nothing was hidden behind their smiles and they were just trying to survive—working long hours and putting on a happy face. The waiters and assistant waiters and stewards were at the top of the totem pole, since they got tips and thus made much more money than the deckhands and other workers, who receive salaries only. It is also possible that people who interact with passengers are chosen for their gregariousness and were genuinely friendly. In truth, everyone on the crew I ever talked with was pleasant.

Crew members inject a certain theatrical aspect into the cruise experience because they are friendly, polite, and always smiling; however, the crew members' true feelings are known only to them. Perhaps they have become so conditioned to this projected friendliness that they really don't know how they feel.

Members of the *Regal Princess* crew are quartered on the lowest deck levels, in two-bed compartments. They share a bathroom with two other crew members in the next cabin. They are buried, deep in the bowels of the ship, where they can hear the engine and other noises that passengers don't hear. One waiter told us that the crew eats after the passengers have finished dining, which means crew members have breakfast around 10:00 a.m., lunch around 3:00 p.m., and dinner well after 11:00 p.m. Some dining crew members are able to take quick naps between lunch and dinner. For those not involved with the food service, running the ship is a twenty-four-hour matter, which means some crew members are working all night, as with some of the officers (who live on one of the top decks on the ship).

THE SHIP AS A LABYRINTH: A SPECULATIVE THEORY

During the cruise I constantly consulted maps to determine my location and noticed many other passengers doing the same thing. In a sense a ship is a labyrinth, a puzzling maze through which we wander, in search of some lounge or bar, not being certain at times whether we are heading toward the front or the back of the ship.

Jungians suggest that mazes, labyrinths, and corridors symbolize the unconscious. This suggests that psychoanalytically speaking, a cruise ship is a physical manifestation of an individual's unconscious, and that taking cruises is an attempt to come to grips with hidden and unconscious elements in our psyches. Although we take cruises for pleasure, without being aware of what we are doing, our wanderings in ships reflect an unrecognized desire to somehow explore unconscious aspects of our psyches. Some psychoanalytic theorists, associated with Freudian thought, argue that labyrinths are unconscious symbols of women (most likely our mothers) whose sexual organs are both hidden and very complicated. In our unconscious thought cruise ships become mother substitutes (we know ships are female) and make us regress to our childhoods once again.

THE CRUISE TRAVEL AGENT
AS "FAIRY GODMOTHER"

We booked our cruise with a cruise travel agency that ran an advertisement in *The San Francisco Chronicle* announcing round-trip cruises from San Francisco to Alaska. So I called up and eventually booked with one of its agents. The agency is one of the largest cruise travel agencies for Princess (and other) lines. On our cruise there were about 150 passengers who had booked with this agency.

Shortly after we got to our cabin we found that our travel agency had sent us a flowering plant. That was a pleasant surprise. The next day there was a note in the door stating that one of its representatives on board had free sweatshirts for us that would be available the next day. Two days later there was another message from our agency—it was throwing a cocktail party for all the passengers who had booked with them. A couple of days after that, a message informed us that we were invited to a special tour of the galley, for our agency's patrons, and two days after that we were invited to a special tour of the bridge. Finally, when we went to dinner the last evening of the cruise we received a small box of chocolates from the agency. Every time we went to our cabin we always wondered whether there would be another message from our agency.

All of this attention suggests that the woman who runs the cruise agency we used is a very good businesswoman. From a psychoanalytic standpoint, she represents a combination of "the good mother" and "the fairy godmother" who is always looking after us—making sure we had warm clothes to wear (the sweatshirt) and enough to eat and drink (the cocktail party) and giving us many gifts. This "good mother" notion would fit in with my hypothesis that taking cruises is a kind of unconscious regression to childhood. When we disembarked and arrived home, I almost expected a message from our agency telling us they hoped we arrived home safely and asking us to give them a phone call so they can make sure. If our agency functioned as the protective mother, it would seem that the ship's captain, the source of all authority on the ship, is the all-powerful (literally and psychoanalytically speaking) father figure. He was very friendly and seemed to spend all his time chatting with passengers and throwing champagne parties, but we all knew he did much more than that.

CONCLUSION

In this chapter I have used Freudian psychoanalytic theory to interpret a number of different aspects of the cruise-taking experience. In some cases I may have pushed things to an extreme. For many people, notions such as the ones I've applied to cruising probably seem quite far-fetched and ridiculous. However, I would argue that they are unfamiliar with psychoanalytic theory and may find it hard to come to grips with certain things about themselves and thus reject psychoanalytic thought as absurd, except when they have psychological problems and need therapy.

Freud explains the hostility people feel toward psychoanalytic thought by arguing that people use various defense mechanisms to avoid coming to grips with their unconscious drives. One is mechanism repression, held by some theorists to be the most basic defense mechanism. Repression involves barring from consciousness various unconscious desires, wishes, and memories; a second defense mechanism is suppression, which involves putting out of the mind and consciousness something an individual finds painful. A third defense mechanism, similar to the other two, is called avoidance and refers to our unwillingness to deal with certain distressing subjects because they are connected to unconscious sexual or aggressive impulses. It would be extremely interesting to see what Freud would have made of the cruising phenomenon.

And yes, I know that Freud said, "Sometimes a cigar is only a cigar!" The flip side of that comment is that sometimes a cigar *isn't* only a cigar!!

Neither its rhetoric or even the informational aspect of its discourse has a decisive effect on the buyer. What the individual does respond to, on the other hand, is advertising's underlying leitmotiv of protection and gratification, the intimation that its solicitations and attempts to persuade are the sign, indecipherable at the conscious level, that somewhere there is an agency (a social agency in the event, but one that refers directly to the image of the mother) which has taken upon itself to inform him of his own desires, and to foresee and rationalize these desires to his own satisfaction. He thus no more "believes" in advertising than the child believes in Father Christmas, but this in no way impeded his capacity to embrace an internalized infantile situation, and to act accordingly. Herein lies the very real effectiveness of advertising, founded on its obedience to a logic which, though not that of the conditioned reflex, is nonetheless very rigorous: a logic of belief and regression.

Jean Baudrillard, *The System of Objects*

Chapter 5

Selling Smooth Sailing:
Advertising and Marketing Cruises

Advertising is meant to sell products, but it also reveals a great deal about the advertiser and the people to whom the products are being sold—that is, the so-called "target audience" for the advertising. In this chapter I deal with cruise advertisements and the brochures (actually rather substantial booklets) that cruise lines send to prospective purchasers of cruises. Remember that a large number of options are open to a traveler, so a cruise line must convince a would-be cruise taker—especially those who haven't cruised before—to give cruises a try. In this chapter I will analyze all the cruise advertisements that appeared in one issue of *Travel + Leisure* (I chose the issue at random) to see what the ads reveal. I will also analyze two brochures sent out by cruise lines at different ends of the spectrum.

INTERPRETING ADVERTISEMENTS

A great deal of research goes into advertising. Advertising agencies employ large numbers of very clever people who use every tool at their disposal—images, music, sound effects, language, various techniques of persuasion—to sell products and services. It is possible to analyze cruise advertisements and gain interesting insights into the cruise industry and the audiences they target. In Chapter 3 we found some statistical information about the demographic nature of people who cruise. Different lines focus their attention on different socioeconomic classes, an example of what is called market segmentation. Obviously, the appeals to someone who intends to spend $800 a day on a cruise will be considerably different from the appeals to someone who plans on spending $80 a day.

The excerpt from Jean Baudrillard, an eminent French social scientist, points out how subtly advertising works. Nobody believes in advertising, per se, but everyone (with few exceptions) is affected by it. Baudrillard's thesis, that advertising works by facilitating regression in people, fits in with my discussion of the regressive aspects of cruising in Chapter 4.

Advertisements are incredibly complex *texts*. This term is used in academic studies for works of any kind, such as print advertisements, television commercials, films, plays, and novels. Advertisements appeal to our rational minds, on one level, but they also attempt to stir things in our unconscious that, if Freud, Jung, and other psychoanalytic theorists are correct, shape our conscious minds and our decision making. Jung (1968) suggested that we tend to overestimate the role of willpower and mistakenly assume that nothing can happen to our minds that we do want to happen. He is alluding to the power of the unconscious in shaping our behavior. This notion explains why people often say that they are "aware" of advertising but insist that they are not influenced by it.

Advertisements can be seen in terms of the metaphor I used for the psyche—the iceberg with the tip reflecting the consciousness, the preconscious located to about six feet below the surface, and the unconscious in the dark areas that we cannot see and cannot access. Advertisements (and all kinds of messages) affect these three realms, which suggests that many of the decisions we make are based upon imperatives lodged in the unconscious realms of our psyche. That is why Freud said "where id was there ego shall be," meaning we should find ways to allow our egos (the rational aspects of our psyches), to shape our behavior instead of our ids or unconscious elements.

In *Culture and the Ad: Exploring Otherness in the World of Advertising,* William M. O'Barr discusses an experiment in which he asked his students at Duke University to examine travel photographs. He writes (1994, pp. 103-104)

> What the Duke students found as a result of their research was confirmation of our suspicions about the relationship between advertisements and travel photographs. They found that tourists seek out not the Japanese but the Japanesy, and they photograph it. These iconographic representations of otherness—whether Geisha girls and pagodas, San Blas women sewing *molas,* or peasants picking coffee beans—validate expectations about what

is to be seen. What would Egypt be without the pyramids, London without the House of Parliament, or Sydney without its opera house? Photographic trophies of tourists standing in front of such sights seem to be essential objectives of modern travel for foreign destinations. These photographs verify that the tourist went, saw, and captured the experience on film.

Travel advertisements color the notions of tourists as to what they should see and what they should expect. We see foreign countries through the "templates" that travel advertising provides us.

In addition, cruise advertising supplies rationales for taking cruises. When I discussed cruising with my fellow passengers on the *Regal Princess,* many of them repeated the slogans and messages they had learned from cruise advertising, such as, "you only have to unpack once" or "you're free to do whatever you want."

In the following section a rather comprehensive list of topics one might consider in analyzing a print advertisement is presented. It has been adapted for cruise advertising from my book *Ads, Fads and Consumer Culture.* Different ads require the use of different topics and methods of analysis and no analysis of a print advertisement will use all of them.

WHAT CAN BE ANALYZED
IN A PRINT ADVERTISEMENT?

Imagine a print advertisement showing a photograph of a man and a woman, a tray with breakfast on it, and some textual material on a cruise ship. Following is a list of possible topics to consider in analyzing the advertisement.

1. How would you describe the design of the advertisement? Do we find axial balance or an asymmetrical relationship among the elements in the advertisement?
2. How much copy is there relative to the amount of pictorial matter? Is this relationship significant in any respect?
3. Does the advertisement contain a great deal of blank (white) space or is it full of graphic and textual material?
4. At what angle is the photograph shot? Do we look up at the people in the advertisement? Do we look down at them from a

height? Or do we look at them from a shoulder-level position? What significance does the angle of the shot have? What views of cruise ships are offered?

5. How is the photograph lit? Does the photo contain a great deal of light or a little light and very dark shadows (chiaroscuro lighting)? What is the mood found in the advertisement?

6. If the photograph is in color, which colors dominate? What significance do these colors have?

7. How would you describe the people in the advertisement? Consider such matters as facial expression, hair color, hair length, hair styling, fashions (clothes, shoes, eyeglasses design, and jewelry), various props (a drink), body shape, body language, race, ethnicity, gender, age, signs of occupation, signs of educational level, relationships suggested between the male and female, and objects in the background.

8. What is happening in the advertisement? What does the "action" in the photo suggest? Assume that we are seeing one moment in an ongoing narrative. What is this narrative and what does it reveal about the two figures? How do the cruise ship and the sea play a role in the advertisement?

9. Are any signs or symbols evident in the photograph? If so, what role do they play? How are images of cruise ships used? Images of luxury?

10. In the textual material, how is language used? What arguments are made or implied about the people in the photograph and about cruises—the product being advertised? That is, what rhetorical devices are used to attract readers and stimulate desire for cruises? Does the advertisement use associations or analogies or something else to make its point?

11. What typefaces are used in the textual parts of the advertisement? What importance do the various typefaces have? (Why these typefaces and not other ones?)

12. What are the basic "themes" in the advertisement? How do these themes relate to the story implied by the advertisement? What is being said about cruises?

13. What aspect of cruising is being advertised? Who is the target audience for this product or service? What role does this product or service play in American culture and society? How is cruising "positioned?"

14. What values and beliefs are reflected in the advertisement? Sexual jealousy? Patriotism? Motherly brotherhood of man? Success? Power? Good taste?
15. Is any background information needed to make sense of the advertisement? How does context and common knowledge shape our understanding of the cruise advertisements?

Some ads are more interesting than others, of course, but all ads convey a great deal more than we might imagine. Every aspect of advertisements must be considered as important if we are to analyze an advertisement and "mine" it for its social, cultural, and ideological content. Using the previous list of topics, the cruise advertisements in one issue of a travel magazine will be analyzed.

CRUISE ADVERTISING IN THE AUGUST 2002
TRAVEL + LEISURE *MAGAZINE*

This issue of *Travel + Leisure* magazine featured a readers' poll on "the world's best" hotels, spas, cities, islands, cruises, and airlines, and offered the following rankings for cruises, in order of popularity. I have reorganized this information into the following chart:

Large-Ship Cruise Lines	Small-Ship Cruise Lines
Crystal	Silversea Cruises
Holland America Line	Radisson Seven Seas
Orient Line	Seabourn
Celebrity Cruises	Linblad Expeditions
Princess Cruises	Windstar
Disney Cruise Line	
Royal Caribbean	
Cunard	
P & O Cruises	
Delta Queen	

This list represents the rankings from a poll conducted by the magazine and should be read as an indicator of how those who participated in the poll felt and not necessarily how everyone or even most people who take cruises might rank the various lines.

I found the following cruise line ads in the August 2002 issue of *Travel + Leisure:*

Cruise Line	Size of Advertisement	Words
Royal Olympic Cruises	Full Page	275
Seabourn	Full Page	200
Silversea	Full Page	115
Cunard	Full Page	70
Crystal	Eight Pages (foldout)	600
Princess	Full Page	150
Norwegian	Full Page	125
Radisson Seven Seas	Full Page	175
Orient Lines	One-Third Page	125
Windjammer	Four Square Inches	40

It's obvious that the standard size advertisement for cruise lines is the full-page advertisement. Crystal had an eight-page foldout, which meant they dominated the attention of readers of the magazine. The ads ranged from those with hardly any copy, such as the Cunard QE2 ad (see Figure 5.1), to those with approximately 275 words, such as the Royal Olympic ad (see Figure 5.2).

The Cunard Advertisement

The Cunard advertisement mentions the number of foreign newspapers found on its deck chairs and the amount of caviar it will be serving during the cruise. The appeal is to the opportunity to mingle with an international (twelve foreign newspapers) "world class" group of people, to mingle with the sophisticated and the great—a movie star or some other kind of celebrity, a prime minister, and so on. The image in the ad, in dark brown, is of someone of importance being photographed by the press and the color of the ad is deliberately understated, so as to suggest refinement and significance.

The Cunard line gets its name from Sir Samuel Cunard who was a cofounder in 1839 of the British and North American Royal Mail

FIGURE 5.1. Cunard Cruise Line Advertisement

Sail on the fastest cruise ships.
Add alluring destinations. Sprinkle with fine cuisine.
And savor more of the Mediterranean coast.

The Olympia Voyager and Olympia Explorer have weekly voyages to some of the most beautiful ports of the Mediterranean. Being the fastest cruise ships in the world, you will be able to see more ports and do more in less time.

Royal Olympic's guests have long cherished our renowned Greek hospitality and fine cuisine. For 2002, we have expanded the onboard and offshore experience to include activities such as:

- Enrichment lectures
- Wine tasting
- Culinary demonstrations
- Exciting shore excursions
- Luxurious Spa treatments

Cruising the Mediterranean is even more accessible than ever. With convenient weekly cruises, low air add-ons and value pricing, there's never been a better time to set sail on an adventure like no other.

Call your Travel Agent or Royal Olympic Cruises today at 1-800-872-6400 to reserve your cabin.

Olympia Voyager - Winner of the most significant new built cruise vessel award sponsored by Lloyd's Cruise International

Beyond words

Olympia Voyager
7-day Golden Fleece Cruise
FROM **$858***

Athens • Istanbul • Kusadasi • Patmos
Mykonos • Rhodes • Heraklion • Santorini

Olympia Explorer - Brand New Ship!
7-day Grand Mediterranean Cruise
FROM **$792***

Athens • Corfu • Venice • Dubrovnik
Katakolon • Istanbul • Mykonos • Santorini

Introducing
THE SEAFARING
GOURMET SERIES

In response to our passengers' passion for fine wine and gourmet cuisine, Royal Olympic is proud to introduce its Seafaring Gourmet Series. While at sea, visiting gourmet chefs will be on board to prepare their renowned recipes to be included in the ship's menus. In addition, you'll be able to attend culinary demonstrations as well as food and wine pairing lectures. Learn what wines go best with which dishes. And best of all, sample both during the cruise!

Royal Olympic Cruises
www.royalolympiccruises.com

FIGURE 5.2. Royal Olympic Cruise Line Advertisement

Steam Packet Company, which became known as the Cunard line. The next year, in 1840, Cunard liners began the first regular steamship service across the Atlantic, so he can be looked upon as the "father" of cruising.

The Silversea Advertisement

Compare the design of the Silversea and Seabourn advertisements (Figures 5.3 and 5.4). Both feature wide spacing between the lines of copy—a signifier of sophistication and tastefulness. Spacing between the lines, and the typefaces used, all suggest "class." These design elements suggest to readers that the lines aren't trying to cram as much copy as they can into a given advertisement. Both are similar in their structural components, with arresting images on the top of the page and copy beneath, and then pictures of their ships at the very bottom. The Silversea ad is a bit more daring in that all elements are flush right. The Seabourn ad is more conventionally designed.

The Silversea advertisement starts with a headline in italics and then reads as follows:

A journey above and beyond all expectations . . .

where vibrant cultures are unveiled, and the intoxicating magic of the most longed-for destinations unfolds before you from your veranda suite. All-inclusive fares ensure that virtually every detail is cared for in advance—roundtrip airfare, pre-cruise deluxe hotel accommodations . . . even such extras as Moet and Chandon champagne, an extensive selection of fine wines and spirits, and all gratuities.

It's an extraordinary travel experience voted World's Best by prestigious publications, travel associations, and most notably, past guests.

To experience the world of Silversea, please consult your travel professional. For more information on our innovative global itineraries, visit us online at www.silversea.com or call toll free, 877-724-4318.

A journey above and beyond all expectations ...

where vibrant cultures are unveiled, and the intoxicating magic of the most longed-for destinations unfolds before you from your veranda suite. All-inclusive fares ensure virtually every detail is cared for in advance — roundtrip airfare, pre-cruise deluxe hotel accommodations ... even such extras as Moët & Chandon champagne, an extensive selection of fine wines and spirits, and all gratuities.

It's an extraordinary travel experience voted World's Best by prestigious publications, travel associations and most notably, past guests.

To experience the world of Silversea, please consult your travel professional. For more information on our innovative global itineraries, visit us online at **www.silversea.com** or call toll free, **877-724-4318**.

§SILVERSEA

VOTED WORLD'S BEST Travel + Leisure 3 Years Condé Nast 6 Consecutive Years Robb Report 3 Consecutive Years

FIGURE 5.3. Silversea Cruise Line Advertisement

The *World of Seabourn.*
It's simply off the charts.

Any cruise line can follow a map of Central and South America. But none can follow Seabourn. Our intimate ships bring you closer to a continent of wonders, sailing right into the heart of Central and South America's most captivating ports of call. From native Amazon villages and glacier carved fjords to the never-ending natural wonders of Costa Rica. And we do so in a manner that defies description. Enjoy an ocean view suite, many with balconies. Complimentary wines and spirits. A retractable watersports marina. Open-seating dining with gourmet menus provided by celebrated chef Charlie Palmer. Complimentary Massage Moments℠ on deck and Movies Under the Stars℠. Virtually one crew member per guest. And an Exclusively Seabourn℠ complimentary shore experience with every cruise.

Enjoy Early Booking Savings of up to 40% on 7- to 18-day Central and South America sailings in 2003. For more information and reservations call any travel agent or Seabourn at 1-800-929-9391. Or visit us at **Seabourn.com**. *America Online Keyword: Seabourn.*

All Suites, many with Balconies

Complimentary Open Bar

The Yachts of Seabourn.
INTIMATE SHIPS. UNCOMPROMISING LUXURY.

Asia · India · Africa · Europe · Caribbean · The Americas

SEABOURN SEABOURN PRIDE · SEABOURN SPIRIT · SEABOURN LEGEND

Seabourn Cruise Line is a proud member of World's Leading Cruise Lines ℠.
Certain conditions apply.

FIGURE 5.4. Seabourn Cruise Line Advertisement

There is an image of a cruise liner in a small two square inch black and white photo and then at the bottom of the page, in very small type, we read:

> Voted World's Best *Travel + Leisure* 3 Years *Condé Nast* 6 Consecutive years Robb Report 3 Consecutive Years

Notice the language used in the Silversea advertisement. Phrases such as "vibrant cultures," "intoxicating magic," "longed-for destinations," and "extraordinary travel experience voted World's Best by prestigious publications" all suggest that a Silversea cruise is for world-class individuals who demand, and will get nothing less than a "world's best" cruise experience in "the world of Silversea." Silversea is selling more than a cruise; it is selling a world in which everything is taken care of and, in principle, all needs are anticipated and dealt with. As we will see in Chapter 6, which has reviews of several cruises, not everyone agrees with Silversea's claim to being "world class."

The Seabourn Advertisement

Like Silversea, Seabourn is also selling a "world." The advertisement reads as follows:

> The World of Seabourn
> It's simply off the charts.

This copy is found on an image, in a muted brown color, of a man and a woman in a canoe exploring a jungle river or stream.

> Any cruise line can follow a map of Central and South America. But none can follow Seabourn. Our intimate ships bring you closer to a continent of wonders, sailing right into the heart of Central and South America's most captivating ports of call. From native Amazon villages and glacier carved fjords to the never-ending natural wonders of Costa Rica. And we do so in a manner that defies description. Enjoy an ocean view suite, many with balconies. Complimentary wines and spirits. A retractable watersports marina. Open-seating dining with gourmet menus provided by celebrated chef Charlie Palmer. Complimentary massage moments on deck and Movies Under the Stars. Virtu-

ally one crew member per guest. And an Exclusively Seabourn complimentary shore experience with every cruise.

To the right of the text are two tiny images—one of a suite with a balcony and one of a martini glass reading, "Complimentary Open Bar." Then below, in a band, is an image of a Seabourn ship and to the right in the same italic face as in the headline

The Yachts of Seabourn
Intimate Ships Uncompromising Luxury

Seabourn is selling luxury but also wonder and adventure that is not available, according to its claims and the implications of it advertisement, to people who take conventional cruises, thanks to Seabourn's "intimate ships" that can sail right into the heart of Central and South America. Like other luxury lines, it has only suites, serves gourmet food, complimentary wine and spirits, and has open seating. Seabourn promises "uncompromising luxury," with attention to passengers' needs, due to its crew-to-passenger ratio of approximately one to one. This is a very high ratio of crew to passengers. In most cruise ships the ratio is closer to one crew member to three passengers.

The appeal, as in the Silversea advertisement, is to people who want luxury but also want adventure and a rich and rewarding experience. Silversea promises "a journey above and beyond all expectations" and Seabourn promises an adventure that is "simply off the charts." Silversea trumpets its ranking as "world's best" and Seabourn promises "uncompromising luxury" thanks to its "virtually one crew member per guest." Both are fighting for that small percentage of people who take super luxury cruises and who expect something beyond what traditional cruise lines offer.

The Princess Advertisement

The Princess ad (Figure 5.5) also has a great deal of white (empty) space in it and is balanced around the center of the page. It actually has very little copy, except for six lines at the very bottom of the page. It uses the famous Princess logo—the image of a woman whose hair becomes waves, and it also uses a curiosity—a lowercase "i" in the phrase *"where i belong."* The ad contains only one sentence:

i want a once-in-a-lifetime cruise at a once-in-a-lifetime *price.*

FIGURE 5.5. Princess Cruise Line Advertisement

The image in the center of the ad, in what resembles a porthole, shows a smiling waiter serving exotic-looking drinks to a pleased, thirtyish couple sitting on a deck. At the very bottom is the standard image of a ship seen from underneath and in front of the bow. But the design of the ad is not sophisticated and does not have the quality "look" of the ads for Seabourn and Silversea.

What is the significance of using a lowercase italicized *"i"*? It could be a simple attempt to attract attention, but it could also suggest a sense of informality and ease that one might find on Princess ships. Notice that "want" and "price" also are in italics. The *i want* suggests someone's desires but it is also a command. The italicized *price* deals with the object of the reader's desire—a once-in-a-lifetime cruise at a once-in-a-lifetime price, suggesting the price of this remarkable cruise is something that will only be this inexpensive once in a lifetime.

The Norwegian Line Advertisement

The Norwegian line ad (Figure 5.6) is divided into three parts: the top image shows a Hawaiian seascape, with the words "Island hop in Hawaii. Unpack once." A green band with copy appears in the middle, and the bottom shows an overhead shot of the Norwegian Star steaming ahead in calm seas. The copy of the ad is of particular interest, in that it makes many of the appeals cruise lines make in their advertising. The headline and copy follow:

Feel free to explore the best of Hawaii aboard the brand new Norwegian Star.

Only NCL gives you the freedom to experience more of Hawaii from the comfort of your own ship with *Freestyle Cruising* all year long. Unpack just once and enjoy four spectacular Hawaiian islands, plus the remote Pacific paradise of Fanning Island. And only NCL offers a brand new ship in Hawaii year-round. Norwegian Star features 10 restaurants, 13 lounges and an incredible selection of recreation, entertainment, and activities. So if you really want to relax, you'd better hop to it. For reservations, see your travel professional or for more information call 1 800 327 7030 or visit www.ncl.com.

Norwegian Cruise Line. Freestyle cruising. Feel Free. Hawaii. Kauai. Oahu. Maui. Fanning Island.

FIGURE 5.6. Norwegian Cruise Line Advertisement

Notice that the ad uses terms involving the word "free" five times: "feel free" (twice), "Freestyle Cruising" (twice), and "freedom to experience" (once). The notion that passengers on NCL ships will be "free" is certainly the most basic appeal in the copy, and deals with the problem mentioned earlier that passengers are afraid of being confined and regimented on cruise ships. The copy makes other standard cruising appeals: first, you have to unpack only once; second, the ship is brand new; third, the ship has ten restaurants so passengers can feel free to eat where they want and when they want; there are many recreation and entertainment activities; and four, on NCL cruises passengers can relax.

Curiously, after informing passengers that they will be free and that they can relax on the Norwegian Star, the ad tells readers that "you'd better hop to it" and make a reservation. The "hop to it" line suggests a kind of informality and casualness that readers can expect to find on NCL ships, but it is also a command, disguised somewhat by its colloquial nature. It is possible to interpret the "feel free" phrase as having a subtle imperative nature to it. Conventionally, "feel free" is something we say to people to put them at ease, but it is also, at the same time, a command. A subtext of regimentation and compulsion hides beneath the text that stresses freedom all the time.

The Crystal Advertisement

The Crystal advertising section—an eight-page foldout—starts off with an arresting image. The first page displays an overhead shot of three officers, resplendent in their white uniforms, walking toward the reader on a gorgeous teak deck. Two-thirds of the page is devoted to the brilliant blue sea and moderate waves that are crashing against the boat leaving a path of white foam. The only words on the page are "Crystal Cruises" on the very top, and below it, "More space." Another page, depicting the food service, has five different food images, and the words "More restaurants." A third page, with a close-up of a croissant, a glass of orange juice, and coffee service on a tray (with a blurred image behind it) has "More verandahs." A fourth page has different shots of smiling people—a cabin stewardess, a young person, and an officer with a guest.

The central section of the foldout is a two-page spread with the title "Sometimes more is more. Introducing Crystal Serenity." This is an allusion to the famous statement attributed to the Dutch architect Mies van der Rohe, "Less is more." There is a two-page side view of the *Serenity* with columns of copy dealing with accommodations, evening dining venues, entertainment venues, enrichment and learning lounges, spas, and fitness venues. Finally, a calendar page lists the various Crystal cruises in 2003. The size and expense of this advertisement is, itself, a statement, and so are the images and copy found in the eight pages—all of which are designed to reinforce Crystal's image as a "luxury" line for sophisticated world travelers who demand the best and are willing to pay for it.

The Radisson Seven Seas Advertisement

The Radisson ad (Figure 5.7), also in muted colors (a signifier of class and sophistication), is composed of six panels: two have text, one has images of two cruise ships, one has a picture of a suite with a large window and balcony and a view of the ocean, one shows someone's legs covered with a towel, and one is a close-up of a bowl on a table with a tablecloth with fancy embroidering. The text in the upper-right-hand corner functions as a headline:

Finally, a sequel
—AS EXCITING—
AS THE ORIGINAL.

Then, in the upper-left-hand corner, in white type against a brown background, we read:

While the 700-guest Seven Seas Voyager may take much of the look, elegance and sense of space from her hugely popular sister ship, she's very much her own girl.

Her suites offer private balconies, more than 350 square feet of comfort, marble-appointed bathrooms and separate showers. Her four restaurants range from casual to Le Cordon Bleu, each with its own atmosphere, charm and cuisine.

Elegance and luxury, certainly; attention to detail and impeccable attentive service, naturally. But always delivered with an attitude that is comfortable and distinctly unstuffy. And all gratuities are included.

To find out more about our inaugural voyages to the Mediterranean, the British Isles, Scandinavia and Russia, visit us at www.rssc.com or call 866-284-4049. For reservations, call an RSSC cruise expert at 866-295-7705. Do it today.

And don't miss your chance to be among the first to sail her.

The panel with the two drawings of the ships informs us that the all-suite, all-balcony Seven Seas Voyager will be launched in April 2003.

The copy in this ad is full of words that imply taste and sophistication: elegance, luxury, marble-appointed, Le Cordon Bleu, impeccable . . . but this is balanced by "distinctly unstuffy." That is, people who cruise on Radisson ships take "attention to detail and impeccable, attentive service" for granted, but this service, the advertisement tells us, is friendly and not intimidating. These Radisson ships are classless, all upper-class, we might say, since Radisson cruises are expensive and reserved, in a sense, for the socioeconomic elites who can afford to take these cruises.

Consider what we don't find in this ad: no mention of entertainment or activities or that kind of thing. The people who take Radisson cruises, and those on other luxury lines, know what they will be getting and don't have to be told about trivial details. The ad ends with two commands: "Do it today" and "don't miss your chance to be among the first to sail her." The appeal to be among the first to sail one of these ships is incongruent with the rest of the ad; people who take Radisson cruises aren't influenced by this kind of an appeal, which seems more likely to attract middle-class people.

The Royal Olympic Cruise Advertisement

This ad starts with three lines of text at the very top—in white type against a dark blue background:

Sail on the fastest cruise ships.
Add alluring destinations. Sprinkle with fine cuisine.
And savor more of the Mediterranean coast.

FIGURE 5.7. Radisson Seven Seas Cruises Advertisement

It reads like a recipe, though it has a number of veiled commands in it: (you must) "sail," (you must) "add," (you must) "sprinkle" and what you get is a "savory" cruise.

The ad contains three images: one of a Royal Olympic cruise ship, one of a tourist spot, presumably on a Greek island, and one of Venice. Below the images is a large panel, divided in two by a line, with text on both sides. The text on the left side of the panel reads as follows:

> The Olympia Voyager and Olympia Explorer have weekly voyages to some of the most beautiful ports of the Mediterranean. Being the fastest ships in the world, you will be able to see more ports and do more in less time.
>
> Royal Olympic's guests have long cherished our renowned Greek hospitality and fine cuisine. For 2002, we have expanded the onboard and offshore experience to include activities such as:
>
> Enrichment lectures
> Wine tasting
> Culinary demonstrations
> Exciting shore excursions
> Luxurious Spa treatments
>
> Cruising the Mediterranean is even more accessible than ever. With convenient weekly cruises, low air add-ons and value pricing, there's never been a better time to set sail on an adventure like no other.

After text concerning contacting a travel agent is a photo of an award and then the following:

> Olympia Voyager—Winner of the most significant new built cruise vessel awards sponsored by Loyd's Cruise International.

Below this is a panel with white letters on a light-blue background:

G R E E C E
Beyond words

In tiny type, below these words is information about the port charges, which run between $165 and $175. This means that seven-day cruises on Royal Olympic lines end up costing approximately $1,050 to $1,100 for a seven-day cruise. This is not terribly expensive, as cruises go, but much more expensive than many seven-day cruises in the Caribbean, which can be as cheap as a few hundred dollars at certain times.

In the right-hand panel is information about the ports of call and costs of the cruises of the Olympia Voyager (from $858) and Olympia Explorer (from $792). Then below this we find:

Introducing the Seafaring Gourmet Series

In response to our passengers' passion for fine wine and gourmet cuisine, Royal Olympic is proud to introduce its Seafaring Gourmet Series. While at sea, visiting gourmet chefs will be onboard to prepare their renowned recipes to be included in the ship's menu. In addition, you'll be able to attend culinary demonstrations as well as food and wine pairing lectures. Learn what wines go best with which dishes. And best of all, sample both during the cruise!

This advertisement, more than any other, looks like a hodgepodge, with many different typefaces, panels, images, and so on. It reflects a different aesthetic sensibility from the other cruise ads. It is an advertisement that is involved in providing information and is not terribly concerned, it would seem, about projecting an aura of sophistication or refinement.

Greece, it tells us, is "beyond words." It is selling the "magic" of Greece—which means it is capitalizing on films such as *Zorba the Greek* and all the spectacular images readers might have seen of the Greek islands in travel magazines, travel brochures, and other publications. Advertisements such as the Royal Olympic ad may not be terribly satisfying from an aesthetic point of view, but they may be very effective.

COMMONALITIES IN THESE CRUISE
ADVERTISEMENTS

Each of these advertisements presented readers with compelling arguments for taking cruises and also provided beautiful images, though there were differences between the market segments to which the different lines were appealing. Collectively, they all were selling cruising and dreams that readers had of "magic" moments as their cruise ships pulled into beautiful islands with spectacular beaches or interesting and fascinating ports of call. The ads also promised extraordinary dining experiences to satisfy the cruisers' "passion," to use a term from the Royal Olympic ad, for fine wines and gourmet cuisine.

Cruise advertisements, like many advertisements, are full of superlatives. These superlatives give potential cruise takers very high expectations of what they will experience on the cruise—expectations that, in some cases, may not be met, leading to a sense of disillusionment. This disillusionment tends to be focused on a particular ship and cruise, and not with cruising in general. Generally speaking, most passengers are satisfied with their cruises and first-time cruisers often state that they intend to take another cruise. Two things are apparent: first, readers of advertisements discount the superlatives and second, the experiences passengers have on cruises are generally positive ones.

Collectively, the ads were selling various attributes of cruising, while individually they were selling the particular features of their cruise line. The cruise industry is highly segmented, ranging from relatively inexpensive cruises to luxury and perhaps even super-luxury ones. These magazine ads contrast considerably with the travel agency cruise ads one generally sees in Sunday travel sections of newspapers. These ads might show a generic image of a cruise ship, mention a particular cruise and ports of call, tell which cruise line is offering the cruise (sometimes, however, they don't tell which line is involved), provide the dates when various sailings will be offered, and a price. These newspaper ads are for people who have done some cruising. The most important matters for them are the name of the cruise line, the dates of the cruises, where the cruises go, and the prices. The newspaper ads are much different, and are closer to magazine cruise ads, though the newspaper cruise ads are generally in black and white.

Many of the advertisements contained thinly veiled commands, such as "hop to it" or "don't miss your chance to be the first to sail her." These commands are subtle and don't read overtly like commands, but they are, in fact, commands—the kind we find in many ads. One of the cardinal rules of advertising is "get people to do something, to take some action" after you've attracted their attention and stimulated their desire.

TWO CRUISE LINE BROCHURE (CATALOG) COVERS

Following is an analysis of two cruise line brochures, one by Carnival lines and one by Seabourn, which is owned by Carnival. Carnival is described in *Selling the Sea* (Dickinson and Vladimir, 1997) as falling in the contemporary category and Seabourn is in the luxury category . . . or perhaps even super-luxury?

The Seabourn catalog is an elegant 106-page booklet with a thin transparent sheet with two champagne glasses on it, through which you can see the cover of the catalog. The cover is very formal, in axial balance and full of white space. The top of the page reads:

2003
The Yachts of Seabourn
Intimate Ships   Uncompromising Luxury
Seabourn Pride   Seabourn Spirit   Seabourn Legend

This is followed by about five inches of an orange sky—presumably a sunset—and then a large side-view image of a Seabourn yacht. Underneath this are the various places Seabourn goes:

Mediterranean and Atlantic Isles   Scandinavia, The Baltic and Russia   Asia, India and Africa   South America   Costa Rica, Belize and Panama Canal   Caribbean   Canada and Colonial America   Transatlantic.

From a design point of view, the formal or axial balance, and the simplicity and emptiness of the cover are all signifiers of sophistication and upper-class taste. The plastic sheet with the imbedded champagne glasses suggests that this brochure was expensive to produce and ties champagne and all its connotations of luxury and joyful celebration to the line. In semiotic jargon, the use of associations to convey meanings is called *metonymy*. Advertisements sell by using metonymy (associations) and *metaphors* (analogies).

The Carnival cover is much different. The cover of this 141-page brochure shows a three-quarter photo (head to knees) of a woman in her thirties wearing a bathing suit and pants over it, smiling happily and running on the beach. She is carrying a large yellow beach towel with green stripes, and behind her, chasing her playfully, is a male of the same approximate age. He is wearing a shirt and is barefoot. The only text on the cover reads:

Carnival
30 Years of Fun
2002-2004 3 to 16 day cruise vacations

The Carnival cover image depicts fun and pleasure—what people who take Carnival cruise vacations can expect. This image tells us that Carnival cruises are for people who want fun. The man and woman on the cover look like ordinary Americans in their thirties and not like the models one sometimes finds in cruise ads—gorgeous women with four percent body fat posing with handsome and distinguished-looking (gray hair, well-tailored suits) middle-aged men. On an inside page the brochure reads, "We didn't invent fun. We just perfected it." Most of the photographs in this brochure are of people in their twenties, thirties, and forties having a wonderful time. They are all smiling and radiating happiness. It is assumed that average people can identify with the figures on the cover of the catalog.

CONCLUSION

This examination of a set of cruise advertisements from *Travel + Leisure* and the covers of the Seabourn and Carnival catalogs offers insights into the appeals different cruise lines make as they seek to attract their target audiences. The most common themes in all of the advertisements involve luxury and exceptional experiences. Except for the luxury and super-luxury lines, such as Seabourn and Silversea, the lines all emphasize gourmet food, freedom, adventure, fun, and pleasure.

Bob Dickinson and Andy Vladimir argue that (1997, p. 218) passengers don't "play back" the positioning found in advertisements. They interviewed 150 passengers, selected at random, on five cruise ships. They discovered that passengers talk about fine food and entertainment on many different lines. Ocean cruise takers, they suggest, differentiate between the cruise lines based on the advertising they have been exposed to, which gives each line a particular identity and personality in their minds.

In other words, cruise lines use advertising to shape our notion of "brand personalities" and these notions actually affect the way we experience their cruises. The advertising gives people expectations and the actual cruise experience either reinforces these expectations or disappoints them. Dickinson and Vladimir (1997) suggested that the people they interviewed did not "play back" the positioning of the line, but they probably did play back the reasons for taking cruises. Since so many passengers take more than one cruise, the expectations cruise takers have are generally realized.

The Internet is a network of networked computers. Its origins are in the US military, seeking ways of protecting information sources and communication by dispersing and fragmenting necessary networks. Its growth was mainly fostered in American universities, but take-off came with the development of the World Wide Web in the early 1990s, providing a relatively simple way of negotiating the Internet by constructing "pages" of on-screen material in the form of hypertext links. Find a page, and on it will be links (usually indicated by blue underlined words, or by graphic symbols) which, if clicked with a mouse pointer, will take you to yet another "page" where the information you seek might be located. . . . One of the most important tools for using the Internet is what are known as "search engines." These are programs designed to search robotically the millions of "pages" held on computers linked to the Internet to find material you need. They are the catalogue of the Internet, but with none of the librarian's informed discretion, or the sensitivity to users' needs in a good library catalogue. However, these tools are a vital entry point for the new user. Their attraction is their simplicity of use, by means of "key words" or phrases, and the often quirky serendipity they encourage, like reading meanderingly through a pile of old newspapers.

David Deacon, Michael Pickering, Peter Golding, and Graham Murdock, *Researching Communications*

Chapter 6

Cruising (on) the Internet

It's a curious thing that we use the metaphor of "cruising" for searching the Internet for information or whatever we are looking for at a given Web site. When we take cruises we stop at one port and then another. The same applies to our searches on the Internet; we go to one Web site after another, but seldom stay very long at any one. But there is a difference between ocean cruising, which is a form of traveling, and searching the Internet, which suggests that someone is looking for something in particular. Travel for pleasure involves going someplace, generally moving around from one place to another, and seeing the "sights." Tours are land-based forms of travel that often use buses, trains, and airplanes for transportation. An ocean cruise has the same purpose but it uses a ship to move from port to port, though in some cases it uses buses or trains for short excursions to sites of interest.

The term "cruise" comes from the Latin term *crux* which means cross. Commonly defined as sailing from place to place for pleasure or in search of something, it has a number of other definitions. The term is often used by homosexuals in reference to looking for a sexual partner but heterosexuals use it as well.

CRUISING THE INTERNET FOR CRUISES

People who are interested in finding cruises often use the Internet to obtain information about a particular cruise and then use a travel agent to take care of the details. Approximately 95 percent of cruises are booked by travel agents who receive around 15 percent of the cost of the cruise from the cruise line. A comparison can be made between cruising the Internet and ocean liner cruising, in general.

Internet Cruising	Cruising on Ships
World Wide Web	World
Web Sites	Ports (1,800 visited by cruise ships)
Search Engine	Travel Agent
Mouse	Ship

We use search engines to find Web sites with information about cruise lines, the cruises they offer, prices, and other useful information. To get an idea of how many Web sites deal with cruising, I called up Google (a search engine) and typed in "cruises" in the search box. In a few seconds it listed 2,960,000 Web sites that have the word "cruises" in them. I then used Google to see how many Web sites there were with topics related to cruises and found the following:

Cruises	2,960,000
Travel	53,200,000
Travel and Cruises	1,230,000
Cruise Travel Agents	1,810,000
Cruise Consolidators	9,020
Cruise Lines	759,000

Obviously, an enormous number of Web sites are devoted to cruising.

CATEGORIES OF CRUISE-RELATED WEB SITES

A number of different categories of Web sites devoted to cruising exist. Some of the more important of these are:

- *Cruise line Web sites.* These are specific Web sites for all the cruise lines such as Carnival, Princess, Seabourn, and Royal Caribbean that supply information about the lines and about various sailings.
- *Travel agencies.* There are general travel agencies, which book airline tickets and other forms of travel in addition to cruises, and there are cruise-only travel agencies. Because I'm inter-

ested in studying cruises I provide my name to a number of different cruise travel agencies and every week I receive messages about "hot deals" on cruises and related information. Some cruise travel agency sites, such as CruiseMates.com, carry bulletin boards, news about the cruise industry, reviews of new boats, and so on.

- *Sites devoted to particular ships.* When I called up Google and typed in *Regal Princess* I found close to 12,000 sites that had material on the *Regal Princess.* I searched for information about the *Regal Princess* before I took my cruise because I wanted to get an idea of what kind of a ship it was.
- *Evaluation sites.* These sites, such as Epinions.com, rank cruise lines and ships and carry reviews from people who have taken a particular cruise. Some sites also contain reviews of a ship or a cruise from a professional travel writer.

Some cruise travel sites had bulletin boards and similar places where there were many reviews of trips people had taken. These reviews were sometimes written as diaries; some were critiques; and often a combination of the two appeared. Many reviews of a particular trip were quite long and detailed. It is not unusual to find opposing views of a ship on the same site; one person loved the cruise and wrote a glowing review and another person hated the same trip, thought the food was terrible, and vowed never to cruise with that line again.

Following are examples of the information on two Internet cruise sites showing the range of information available and what is important to people who take cruises. I will then offer a couple of reviews; these reviews are similar to interviews one might conduct to get information about cruising and gain insights into what cruisers like and dislike. One difficulty is that many reviews give only brief information about a given ship and are mostly about ports people visited and what they did.

INTERNET CRUISE-ONLY TRAVEL AGENCIES

Of the thousands of travel agencies available, I chose a couple of typical ones—Cruise Critic and CruiseMates—to show what topics these Web sites cover (see <www.cruisecritic.com> and <www. cruisemates.com>). On these sites you find the following lists of topics:

CruiseCritic.com	CruiseMates.com
Home	Message boards
Contents	Photo galleries
Rate a ship	Meet on board
Ship reviews	Ship poll
Ship itineraries	Families
Cruise news	Teens
Cruise bargains	Singles
Bargain finder	Contests and games
Classified ads	First cruisers
Newsletter	Member reviews
	Chat
	Gay and lesbian

This list covers the basic questions that cruise agencies think a person interested in cruising might have, but they also indicate trends in cruising such as teen cruising and gay and lesbian cruising. Between the two sites you can find just about anything you might want to know about cruising, such as itineraries, bargains, what to expect for people who have never cruised before, and information on the cruise industry. The sites also have versions available in foreign languages such as Spanish, French, and German.

CruiseMates.com has a list of cruise reviews sorted by cruise lines. For example:

Carnival Cruise Lines—198 Reviews
Celebrity Cruises—127 Reviews
Princess Cruises—115 Reviews

I thought I might get a tolerably randomized sampling of what these reviews were like by taking the first review for the lines with advertisements in *Travel + Leisure* magazine: Carnival, Crystal, Cunard,

Norwegian, Princess, Radisson, Royal Olympic, Seven Seas, Seabourn, and Silversea cruise lines. But I discovered that all the reviews were positive and so I concluded that this approach wouldn't work.

To get an idea of who is using these Internet cruise Web sites, I went to the press section of CruiseCritic.com and obtained the following information. I have reformulated it in the chart that follows. This data is used by permission of The Independent Traveler, Inc. (n.d.).

Cruise Critic Visitor Information Statistics

Monthly visitors:	750,000	
Annual visitors:	2 million	
Minutes per visit:	Fifteen	
Age of visitors:	58 %	36 to 55
	20%	56 and above
Income:	55%	$75,000
	30%	$100,000 and above
Gender:	63%	Female
	37%	Male
Education:	58%	College
	19%	Postgraduate
Travel history:	48%	Cruise every year
	16%	Cruise two or more times per year
	19%	First-time cruise takers
	89%	Will book a cruise within twelve months
	54%	Have bought travel online
	19%	Have bought a cruise online
	$2,272	Average dollars spent on cruise vacation

Clearly, this site gets an enormous amount of interest from potential cruise takers, who spend approximately fifteen minutes each time they log on. The incomes of these viewers are decidedly in the upper-income levels. Of course, people have been known to exaggerate their income level when taking surveys.

I logged on to different cruise review sites and selected a couple of reviews of luxury lines that I thought were fairly representative of typical reviews. In the first one, the reviewer, who has taken twenty-seven cruises, was asked to rate the ship on which he traveled on more than forty topics, with 100 being the highest possible score for each category. Everyone who wrote a review on this site was asked to rate the ship on these topics. The second review is a longer and more detailed review of a cruise, which doesn't make use of the list used in the first review, but covers a number of the same topics.

Two Cruise Reviews

Following is a review form, which I've adapted from one on the Internet, that lists more than forty different topics to consider when evaluating a cruise. I've replaced the various items in alphabetical order and numbered them, though they aren't that way on the original form. The form asks respondents to rank each item on a scale from one to 100. There were a total of nine reviews of Silversea cruises. One reviewer gave his cruise an overall rating of 100 and others were less generous, giving overall scores from 85 to 100. This form is a modified version of the one found on About.com (n.d.).

1. Air and sea program
2. Beauty salon
3. Beauty salon staff
4. Cabin amenities
5. Cabin comfort
6. Cabin quietness
7. Cabin steward
8. Casino
9. Casino staff
10. Cruise activities
11 Cruise director
12. Cruise staff
13. Deck service
14. Deck space
15. Dining room service
16. Disco/nightclubs
17. Disembarkation

18. Embarkation
19. Entertainment at poolside
20. Entertainment in lounges
21. Entertainment in show lounge
22. Exercise facilities
23. Food at the midnight buffets
24. Food by room service
25. Food in the dining room
26. Food in the lido deck (buffet)
27. Food variety
28. Good for families
29. Good for honeymoon
30. Good for seniors
31. Lounge service
32. Medical facilities
33. Overall cruise value
34. Overall ports of call
35. Private island
36. Ship cleanliness
37. Shops on board
38. Shore excursions value
39. Shore excursions variety
40. Space ratio
41. Stabilization
42. Tender service
43. Wheelchair access

One reviewer stated that it was worth taking the cruise, but he may have been trying to convince himself that he had a better time than he actually had, because he didn't give his cruise very high ratings, in general. He mentions that the afternoon teas were disappointing and that the shore excursions were good, but, as is typical on most lines, greatly overpriced. He adds that he felt a bit cramped on his ship, especially when compared to large luxury cruises he has taken in the past. He also didn't think the tour desk and reception area were very attractive. He reports that he was pleased about the way Silversea treated him and his wife to a bus tour and lunch after they disembarked but felt that on a per-diem basis Silversea cruises are overpriced. He gave his cruise an overall rating of 85.

The next review of a Crystal *Symphony* Panama cruise in October 1997 is quite long and very detailed. The author discusses the various islands visited and other matters, which are not of interest for our purposes. It is informative and it would be of great interest to someone contemplating taking a cruise with the Crystal line and, in particular, on the Crystal *Symphony*. What most impressed the author was the sense of happiness and satisfaction he noticed among the passengers and a sense that everyone was part of one, big, happy family. Passengers on that cruise, he suggests, developed a feeling of "shared contentment" that led to a magical feeling of connectedness and fulfillment (Cruises.com, n.d.). This review was done, it seems, by a professional writer and reviewer rather than by a typical passenger on a cruise.

Analysis of the Reviews

The first reviewer, who had taken twenty-seven cruises before his cruise on the Silversea lines, emerged generally disappointed from the experience and apparently disillusioned with Silversea cruises. He didn't give many of the topics he was asked to evaluate extremely high marks and in his written commentary, he often unfavorably compares Silversea with Crystal lines. The form at the beginning of the first review shows how incredibly complex cruising is—how many different things can go wrong on a cruise—as compared to something rather simple such as spending a night in a hotel or motel and dining in a restaurant.

The second reviewer who sailed on the Crystal *Symphony* was almost ecstatic in his praise of the Crystal line, the ship he was on, and of his experience on the cruise. At the end of the review he discusses the sense of connectedness everyone on the ship felt and comments that on this cruise, the promises of the cruise line brochures, which were full of superlatives and descriptions of wonderful experiences that cruisers would have, were realized.

Bob Dickinson and Andy Vladimir (1997) suggest that among other things, people on cruises are looking to escape from a sense of alienation that they often feel in their everyday lives. They compare a family trip by car and one on a cruise and comment that car vacations don't generate the same sense of community that cruises do.

People who take cruises are, literally speaking, "all in the same boat together," and this can create a sense of relatedness and togetherness that counters the alienation they may experience at times in their everyday lives. Unlike automobile vacations, which aren't radically different from everyday experiences, a cruise is a major departure from everyday life. A significant break with routine occurs when you walk up the gangplank on a ship. While you are on the ship you are having a much different experience from your onshore life, which helps explain why cruises are so satisfying. In a sense, a car trip to a national park is "more of the same" while a cruise is completely different. That explains why the second reviewer mused that "days and days at sea" is one of the best parts of cruising.

CRUISE LINE WEB SITES

Cruise line Web sites aren't particularly interesting—with the exception of the Seabourn Web site, which has music and moving images, and is very elaborate. Cruise line Web sites generally offer information about the cruise company, its various ships, the destinations to which the line cruises (and a calendar listing the dates of the cruises, how long they last, and what they cost), and how to get new brochures and special offers. Because 95 percent of cruises are booked by travel agents, the lines do not push viewers of their Web sites to book with the line, but suggest instead that they contact a travel agent.

These Web sites do enable people who are contemplating booking a cruise to get information that will be helpful to them, and together with the cruise evaluation Web sites, an Internet "cruiser" can get a considerable amount of information about the different lines, various ships, and ports of call, among other things. Before I took our cruise to Alaska, I downloaded numerous reviews of the Princess line and the *Regal Princess.* I also downloaded the Princess line's menu for a typical seven-day cruise. Menus are all, by nature, studies in hyperbole and the Princess menu was that.

A great deal of the selling by cruise lines is done by their brochures, which are full of dazzling pictures of people having a wonderful time as they gaze out at spectacularly beautiful vistas. But those who cruise the Internet can find other sources to counter the powerful sell of the brochures. A person contemplating a cruise on a

Silversea ship might be deterred by reading the review I reprinted while a person thinking about taking a Crystal line cruise would be reassured and motivated to sail on the Crystal *Symphony.*

CONCLUSION

The Internet is a source of information on all kinds of subjects and if the figures for the number of people accessing the CruiseCritic. com site are reliable, huge numbers of people are checking out different kinds of cruise sites and gleaning information from them. However, realize that people who send reviews into such sites are self-selected and unusually motivated. Generally, they are either very happy with their cruise or very unhappy with it; otherwise they wouldn't bother writing a review.

These reviews are an electronic form of word of mouth, which is generally the most powerful determinant when buying a cruise, or anything else. However, it is not unusual to find two reviews of the same cruise (or same ship) which are polar opposites; one person loved everything about the ship and another person hated everything about it. So the Internet can't provide a conclusive answer to someone who is thinking of taking a cruise. Real word of mouth is much better, and for those who know little, cruise travel agents often can provide reliable information.

Why is travel so exciting? Partly because it triggers the thrill of escape, from the constriction of the daily, the job, the boss, the parents. "A great part of the pleasure of travel," says Freud, "lies in the fulfillment of . . . early wishes to escape the family and especially the father." The escape is also from the traveler's domestic identity, and among strangers a new sense of selfhood can be tried on, like a costume. The anthropologist Claude Lévi-Strauss notes that a traveler takes a journey not just in space and time (most travel being to places more ancient than the traveler's home) but "in the social hierarchy as well"; and he has noticed repeatedly that arriving in a new place, he has suddenly become rich (travelers to Mexico, China, or India will know the feeling). The traveler's escape, as least since the Industrial Age, has also been from the ugliness and racket of Western cities, and from factories, parking lots, boring turnpikes, and roadside squalor.

Paul Fussell (Ed.), *The Norton Book of Travel*

Chapter 7

Notes from a Cruise Journal

In 1999 my wife and I took a seven-night cruise from Los Angeles to Puerto Vallarta and back on the *Song of America*. After I wrote *Ocean Travel and Cruising* I read over the journal I kept while on the cruise. I was struck by the similarity between many of the ideas I dealt with in this book and the thoughts I had about the Puerto Vallarta cruise, and, by implication, cruising in general. What follows is a selection of short passages from the cruise journal I kept when I was on what was advertised to be the last sailing of the *Song of America* in January 1999. I have been keeping journals since 1954 and use them in planning and writing my books. The sociologist in me finds cruises culturally interesting. *Ocean Travel and Cruising* is the ultimate result of that interest.

There's something relaxing about being on the ocean, on a cruise . . . you spend a good deal of time eating . . . and wandering about, reading, etc., away from the routine . . .

I think I'll give up two desserts. . . . People are drinking all kinds of exotic drinks in strange-looking glasses . . . and gambling away. I imagine they're having a very good time. . . . They seem to be. The days stretch out and last forever.

It's a kind of enforced relaxation. . . . There are a lot of things to do. . . . You could keep busy every minute if you want to. I bumped into two women we met during embarkation. . . . They mentioned how time seems to stretch out when one is in a boat . . . it may be because we're out of our usual pattern? Whatever the case, it's quite pleasant. The sunset yesterday was very beautiful.

The show was a wild, Vegas-type show . . . with all kinds of crazy costumes, singing, and dancing . . . an extravaganza. I got a kick out of it. Lots of energy expended.

The waiter said there are 100 cooks on the ship. It has almost 1,500 passengers and a staff of more than 500. A little city. A floating hotel, actually. I think the food's been quite good. The meals are worth quite a lot . . . if you had to pay for them you'd spend a fortune. . . . Still, the lines are doing well so they must make a lot on each passenger.

Now I'm on the ninth deck . . . it's a bit noisy. There's a kind of festive quality . . . I'm on a deck chair surveying the scene. . . . This is a small ship . . . 37,000 tons. I rather like the size . . . it means everything is accessible without much chasing around. Some people are on vacation but many others, especially the retired people, are continually taking cruises . . .

The class level on this boat . . . lots of people seem to be lower-middle class . . . with pockets of who knows what? There are class divisions by boats . . . not by cabins but cruise lines . . .

Our waiter Anthony is twenty-six . . . he's from Bombay. . . . He's been working for Royal Caribbean for five years, he said. If he gets $50 per couple and he serves twenty couples, he makes $1,000 a week. Not bad, but it's very hard work. The woman who serves wine is Hungarian and the assistant waiter is Romanian. There are people from more than fifty countries on this boat.

The waiters work from 6:30 a.m. until midnight most days and a couple of days until 2:30 or 3:00 a.m. . . . when there are midnight buffets. Quite incredible. And they do that for six months, without a day off. Then they have six weeks off—forty-two days—and back they go again for another six months . . . and so on, ad infinitum.

We're moving into our fourth day of the cruise and we're having a good time. . . . It takes a while for you to start relaxing. Now we're both much more relaxed . . . so it will have turned out to be a really good break. A nice way to "get away from it all."

I've been amazed at the number of people who travel constantly . . . as if doomed to travel endlessly. I think it would get boring after a while? I find a week boring . . . but relaxing. Being on a ship is a pleasant experience . . . different from our everyday living . . . a touch of luxury.

Tours offer luxury for the proletariat . . . proletourism?? It's the only opportunity the average person has to have such a luxurious lifestyle . . . everyone on the crew calls my wife Phyllis "madame" and is excessively polite.

Cruises as approximations of paradise. You don't work, you eat very well, everyone knocks themselves out to make you happy. . . . The scenery is often lovely . . . and after a certain number of days you're kicked out. There's also temptation at the gambling casinos.

The ocean is part of the pleasure of cruising. . . . There's something about the ocean that is fascinating . . . perhaps because we emerged from the ocean millions of years ago? Or because it has so many exotic creatures?

Cruises are an interesting "problem" for me . . . the sociologist in me wonders about the occupations, socioeconomic class levels of the people on the cruise. Many of them don't speak English correctly. . . . Maybe some of them are poorly educated but well-to-do?

Tonight's dinner was the best one we had, I think—though others were quite fine as well. . . . It's amazing how the kitchen can cook so many meals for the staff and passengers and have the food taste so good. We went to look at the midnight buffet . . . it was an extravaganza of shaved ice statues, animals made out of cheese and bread, etc. Plus an awesome display of cakes.

The seas are a bit rougher now . . . so people are lurching around. . . . We are in our cabin getting ready to go to bed. . . . We gave our tips to one and all . . . it's almost over. . . . I don't think we'll take another cruise for quite a while. . . . As cruises go, I think this was excellent but I don't think I'm suited to go on cruises. Too much of a good thing!

Quite obviously, my decision to avoid going on cruises because they are "too much of a good thing" didn't last very long, and our cruise on the Princess lines' *Regal Princess* was, my wife and I felt, a much better one than we had on the *Song of America.* This was because we had friends with us on the cruise, but we didn't spend that much time together, interestingly enough. I believe the Princess line offers a better product than we had on the *Song of America.* If you think about it, both ships had approximately the same number of passengers and the *Regal Princess* was twice as big as the *Song of America,* and I think Princess lines might attract a different kind of passenger than Royal Caribbean. The fact that we were on a ten-night cruise also might have had something to do with our feelings about our cruise to Alaska.

In any case, we concluded—when we arrived back in San Francisco—that we would try another cruise in the not-too-distant future. I now believe that a little bit of "too much of a good thing" from time to time isn't so bad!

References

About.Com (n.d.). Cruise Reviews and Trip Reports. Available online at <http://cruises.about.com/cs/cruisereviews/>. Accessed July 22, 2002.

Arnold, Matthew (1951). Culture and Anarchy. In C.F. Harrold and W. Templeman, (Eds.), *English Prose of the Victorian Era.* New York: Oxford University Press.

Bakhtin, Mikhail (1984). *Rabelais and His World.* Bloomington, IN: Indiana University Press.

Baudrillard, Jean (1996). *The System of Objects,* trans. James Benedict. London: Verso.

Berger, Arthur Asa (1997). *Postmortem for a Postmodernist.* Walnut Creek, CA: AltaMira Press.

Berger, Arthur Asa (2003). *Ads, Fads and Consumer Culture: Advertising's Impact on American Character and Society,* Second Edition. Lanham, MD: Rowman and Littlefield.

The Bible Designed To Be Read As Living Literature: The Old and the New Testaments in the King James Version (1951). Arranged and Edited by Ernest Sutherland Bates. New York: Simon and Schuster.

Camus, Albert (1963). *Notebooks, 1935-1942.* New York: Alfred Knopf.

Carnival Cruise Lines (n.d.). Fantastic Food Facts from the "Fun Ship" Fleet. Press release.

Cruise Lines International Association (n.d.). Press Room and Research. Available online at <http://www.cruising.org/press>. Accessed July 26, 2002.

Cruise Lines International Association (n.d.). Profile of the U.S. Cruise Industry. Available online at <http://www.cruising.org/press/sourcebook/profile_cruise_industry.cpm>. Accessed July 14, 2002.

Cruises.Com (n.d.). Cruise Reviews. Available online at <http://www.cruise.com/reviews/reviewers1.html>. Accessed August 2, 2002.

de Saussure, Ferdinand (1966). *A Course in General Linguistics.* New York: McGraw-Hill.

Deacon, David, Michael Pickering, Peter Golding, and Graham Murdock (1999). *Researching Communications: A Practical Guide to Methods in Media and Cultural Analysis.* London: Arnold.

DeNavas-Walt, Carmen and Robert W. Cleveland (2002). *Money Income in the United States: 2001.* Washington, DC: U.S. Government Printing Office. Available online at <http://www.census.gov/prod/2002pubs/p60-218.pdf>. Accessed July 30, 2002.

Dichter, Ernest (2002). *The Strategy of Desire.* New Brunswick, NJ: Transaction Books.

Dickinson, Bob and Andy Vladimir (1997). *Selling the Sea: An Inside Look at the Cruise Industry.* New York: Wiley.

Frisby, David and Mike Featherstone (Eds.) (1997). *Simmel on Culture.* London: Sage Publications.

Frommer's (n.d.). A Few Money-Saving Tips. Available online at <http://www.frommers.com/destinations/bahamas/0205036232.html>. Accessed August 3, 2002.

Fussell, Paul (Ed.) (1987). *The Norton Book of Travel.* New York: W.W. Norton.

Goeldner, Charles R., J.R. Brent Ritchie, and Robert W. McIntosh (2000). *Tourism: Principles, Practices, Philosophies* (Eighth Edition). New York: Wiley.

The Independent Traveler (n.d.). About Us: Demographics. Available online at <http://www.independenttraveler.com/aboutus/demographics.cfm>. Accessed July 18, 2002.

Jung, Carl G. (Ed.) (1968). *Man and His Symbols.* New York: Dell.

Knotts, Bob (2002). "If It's Tuesday . . ." *Budget Travel* 5(4): 123-124.

Leed, Eric J. (1991). *The Mind of the Traveler: From Gilgamesh to Global Tourism.* New York: Basic Books.

Macbeth, Jim (1980). Ocean Cruising: A Study of Affirmative Deviance. Unpublished dissertation, Murdoch University, Murdoch, Western Australia.

MacCannell, Dean (1976). *The Tourist: A New Theory of the Leisure Class.* New York: Schocken Books.

Milgram, Stanley (1976). "The Image Freezing Machine." *Society* (November/December), 7-12.

O'Barr, William M. (1994). *Culture and the Ad: Exploring Otherness in the World of Advertising.* Boulder, CO: Westview.

Sebeok, T. (Ed.) (1977). *A Perfusion of Signs.* Bloomington: Indiana University Press.

Slater, Shirley and Harry Basch (1997). *Fielding's Alaska Cruises.* Redondo Beach, CA: Fielding Worldwide.

Wood, Robert E. (2000). "Globalization at Sea: Cruise Ships and the Deterritorialization of Capital, Labor, and Place." Paper presented at Eastern Sociological Society, March, Baltimore, MD.

Zeman, J. Jay (1977). Peirce's Theory of Signs. In T. Sebeok, (Ed.), *A Perfusion of Signs.* Bloomington: Indiana University Press.

Index

Note: Page numbers followed by the letter "f" indicate figures.

THE HAWORTH HOSPITALITY PRESS®
Hospitality, Travel, and Tourism
K. S. Chon, PhD, Editor in Chief

OCEAN TRAVEL AND CRUISING: A CULTURAL ANALYSIS by Arthur Asa Berger. (2004). "Dr. Berger presents an interdisciplinary discussion of the cruise industry for the thinking person. This is an enjoyable social psychology travel guide with a little business management thrown in. A great book for the curious to read a week before embarking on a first cruise or for the frequent cruiser to gain a broader insight into exactly what a cruise experience represents." *Carl Braunlich, DBA, Associate Professor, Department of Hospitality and Tourism Management, Purdue University, West Lafayette, Indiana*

STANDING THE HEAT: ENSURING CURRICULUM QUALITY IN CULINARY ARTS AND GASTRONOMY by Joseph A. Hegarty. (2003). "This text provides the genesis of a well-researched, thoughtful, rigorous, and sound theoretical framework for the enlargement and expansion of higher education programs in culinary arts and gastronomy." *John M. Antun, PhD, Founding Director, National Restaurant Institute, School of Hotel, Restaurant, and Tourism Management, University of South Carolina*

SEX AND TOURISM: JOURNEYS OF ROMANCE, LOVE, AND LUST edited by Thomas G. Bauer and Bob McKercher. (2003). "Anyone interested in or concerned about the impact of tourism on society and particularly in the developing world, should read this book. It explores a subject that has long remained ignored, almost a taboo area for many governments, institutions, and organizations. It demonstrates that the stereotyping of 'sex tourism' is too simple and travel and sex have many manifestations. The book follows its theme in an innovative and originial way." *Carson L. Jenkins, PhD, Professor of International Tourism, University of Strathclyde, Glasgow, Scotland*

CONVENTION TOURISM: INTERNATIONAL RESEARCH AND INDUSTRY PERSPECTIVES edited by Karin Weber and Kye-Sung Chon. (2002). "This comprehensive book is truly global in its perspective. The text points out areas of needed research—a great starting point for graduate students, university faculty, and industry professionals alike. While the focus is mainly academic, there is a lot of meat for this burgeoning industry to chew on as well." *Patti J. Shock, CPCE, Professor and Department Chair, Tourism and Convention Administration, Harrah College of Hotel Administration, University of Nevada–Las Vegas*

CULTURAL TOURISM: THE PARTNERSHIP BETWEEN TOURISM AND CULTURAL HERITAGE MANAGEMENT by Bob McKercher and Hilary du Cros. (2002). "The book brings together concepts, perspectives, and practicalities that must be understood by both cultural heritage and tourism managers, and as such is a must-read for both." *Hisashi B. Sugaya, AICP, Former Chair, International Council of Monuments and Sites, International Scientific Committee on Cultural Tourism; Former Executive Director, Pacific Asia Travel Association Foundation, San Francisco, CA*

TOURISM IN THE ANTARCTIC: OPPORTUNITIES, CONSTRAINTS, AND FUTURE PROSPECTS by Thomas G. Bauer. (2001). "Thomas Bauer presents a wealth of detailed information on the challenges and opportunities facing tourism operators in this last great tourism frontier." *David Mercer, PhD, Associate Professor, School of Geography & Environmental Science, Monash University, Melbourne, Australia*

SERVICE QUALITY MANAGEMENT IN HOSPITALITY, TOURISM, AND LEISURE edited by Jay Kandampully, Connie Mok, and Beverley Sparks. (2001). "A must-read. . . . a treasure. . . . pulls together the work of scholars across the globe, giving you access to new ideas, international research, and industry examples from around the world." *John Bowen, Professor and Director of Graduate Studies, William F. Harrah College of Hotel Administration, University of Nevada, Las Vegas*

TOURISM IN SOUTHEAST ASIA: A NEW DIRECTION edited by K. S. (Kaye) Chon. (2000). "Presents a wide array of very topical discussions on the specific challenges facing the tourism industry in Southeast Asia. A great resource for both scholars and practitioners." *Dr. Hubert B. Van Hoof, Assistant Dean/Associate Professor, School of Hotel and Restaurant Management, Northern Arizona University*

THE PRACTICE OF GRADUATE RESEARCH IN HOSPITALITY AND TOURISM edited by K. S. Chon. (1999). "An excellent reference source for students pursuing graduate degrees in hospitality and tourism." *Connie Mok, PhD, CHE, Associate Professor, Conrad N. Hilton College of Hotel and Restaurant Management, University of Houston, Texas*

THE INTERNATIONAL HOSPITALITY MANAGEMENT BUSINESS: MANAGEMENT AND OPERATIONS by Larry Yu. (1999). "The abundant real-world examples and cases provided in the text enable readers to understand the most up-to-date developments in international hospitality business." *Zheng Gu, PhD, Associate Professor, College of Hotel Administration, University of Nevada, Las Vegas*

CONSUMER BEHAVIOR IN TRAVEL AND TOURISM by Abraham Pizam and Yoel Mansfeld. (1999). "A must for anyone who wants to take advantage of new global opportunities in this growing industry." *Bonnie J. Knutson, PhD, School of Hospitality Business, Michigan State University*

LEGALIZED CASINO GAMING IN THE UNITED STATES: THE ECONOMIC AND SOCIAL IMPACT edited by Cathy H. C. Hsu. (1999). "Brings a fresh new look at one of the areas in tourism that has not yet received careful and serious consideration in the past." *Muzaffer Uysal, PhD, Professor of Tourism Research, Virginia Polytechnic Institute and State University, Blacksburg*

HOSPITALITY MANAGEMENT EDUCATION edited by Clayton W. Barrows and Robert H. Bosselman. (1999). "Takes the mystery out of how hospitality management education programs function and serves as an excellent resource for individuals interested in pursuing the field." *Joe Perdue, CCM, CHE, Director, Executive Masters Program, College of Hotel Administration, University of Nevada, Las Vegas*

MARKETING YOUR CITY, U.S.A.: A GUIDE TO DEVELOPING A STRATEGIC TOURISM MARKETING PLAN by Ronald A. Nykiel and Elizabeth Jascolt. (1998). "An excellent guide for anyone involved in the planning and marketing of cities and regions. . . . A terrific job of synthesizing an otherwise complex procedure." *James C. Maken, PhD, Associate Professor, Babcock Graduate School of Management, Wake Forest University, Winston-Salem, North Carolina*